WINGS OF RESILIENCE

How to Thrive in the Face of Adversity

MARIAN WEST ULRICH

DOWNLOAD YOUR FREE GIFT!

Read this guide I put together for you, to help you discover the top 5 ways to become more resilient, so you can build the life of your dreams.

Download it at:
https://linktr.ee/WingsofResilienceforLife

Copyright © 2024 by **Marian West Ulrich**

Printed in the United States of America.

All rights reserved. No part of this publication may be reproduced, distributed or transmitted in any form or by any means, including photocopying, recording, or other electronic or mechanical methods, without the prior written permission of the author at marian@wingsofresilienceforlife.com, except in the case of brief quotations embodied in critical reviews and certain other noncommercial uses permitted by copyright law.

Marian West Ulrich
Wilson, North Carolina 27896

Scriptures used in this book are taken from the NEW INTERNATIONAL VERSION (NIV), unless otherwise indicated: Scripture taken from the THE HOLY BIBLE, NEW INTERNATIONAL VERSION ®. Copyright© 1973, 1978, 1984, 2011 by Biblica, Inc.™. Used by permission of Zondervan.

Scriptures marked ESV are taken from the THE HOLY BIBLE, ENGLISH STANDARD VERSION (ESV): Scriptures taken from THE HOLY BIBLE, ENGLISH STANDARD VERSION ® Copyright© 2001 by Crossway, a publishing ministry of Good News Publishers. Used by permission.

Scriptures marked KJV are taken from the KING JAMES VERSION (KJV): KING JAMES VERSION, public domain.

Scriptures marked TM are taken from the THE MESSAGE: THE BIBLE IN CONTEMPORARY ENGLISH (TM): Scripture taken from THE MESSAGE: THE BIBLE IN CONTEMPORARY ENGLISH, copyright©1993, 1994, 1995, 1996, 2000, 2001, 2002. Used by permission of NavPress Publishing Group.

Scriptures marked NLT are taken from the HOLY BIBLE, NEW LIVING TRANSLATION (NLT): Scriptures taken from the HOLY BIBLE, NEW LIVING TRANSLATION, Copyright© 1996, 2004, 2007 by Tyndale House Foundation. Used by permission of Tyndale House Publishers, Inc., Carol Stream, Illinois 60188. All rights reserved. Used by permission.

ISBN 979-8-218-59217-2

Published by 4HG Publishing, LLC www.dakfrederick.com
Edited by Hayes A.
Cover design by Sam

Wings of Resilience: How to Thrive in the Face of Adversity/Marian West Ulrich.—1st ed.

Disclaimer: This publication is designed to provide a source of valuable information for the reader; however, nothing contained in or accessible from this book should be considered as professional advice and is not meant as a substitute for direct expert assistance. The publisher and author has made every effort to ensure that the information in this book is accurate at the time of publication. The content of this book is not guaranteed to be correct, complete, or up-to-date. In regard to the subject matter covered, the publisher and the author assume no responsibility for errors, inaccuracies, omissions, or any other inconsistencies herein and hereby disclaim any liability to any party for any loss, damage, or disruption caused by errors or omissions, whether such errors or omissions result from negligence, accident, or any other cause. The use of this book implies your acceptance of this disclaimer.

TABLE OF CONTENTS

Foreword 1

Introduction 5

Chapter 1 – The Red Rose 7

Chapter 2 – The Most Timely And Perfect Gift From Mother 15

Chapter 3 – One Of The World's Best Dads 19

Chapter 4 – A Sense of Community 23

Chapter 5 – Family Lessons and Family Ties 31

Chapter 6 – Working To Eat 47

Chapter 7 – Working at a Five and Dime Store 57

Chapter 8 – Looking For Love In The Wrong Places 61

Chapter 9 – A Crossroads and a Choice to Make 71

Chapter 10 – What Will I Name Her? 75

Chapter 11 – The Promise: How I Avoided the Welfare Aid Trap 79

Chapter 12 – Job by Day University By Night 85

Chapter 13 – The Wrong Husband 91

Chapter 14 – Houses of Higher Learning 97

Chapter 15 – Professional Business Mom 99

Chapter 16 – The First Right Husband 109

Chapter 17 – Culture Shock 121

Chapter 18 – God Why Do You Take Away The Good Husbands? . 131

Chapter 19 – The Second Promise at Widowhood 143
Chapter 20 – Faith and Hope 151
Life Today 155
Conclusion 157
Epilogue 159
Bible Verses I Stood On 161
Download Your Free Gift! 175
About the Author 177

FOREWORD

By Nana Hinsley and Nina White

Nana Hinsley

In the words of our author, "I HAVE LOST BUT I DID NOT LOSE!" These powerful words encapsulate the spirit of resilience that infuses this extraordinary book. This captivating book reveals the incredible life of a woman who rose from the depths of rock bottom, epitomizing unwavering courage and determination.

Raised in the 1950s during an era of segregation, she faced the unique challenges of being black, a female, a single teenage mother, married, abused, a widow, and a businesswoman-sometimes all at once.

Through it all, her unshakeable faith in God provided her with the strength and resilience to press on. In today's world, where life is darker and harder than ever, where hope is in short supply, her story offers a profound reminder of the power of unwavering determination.

This book is a lifeline—a handbook for those seeking direction and inspiration. As her experiences unfold, readers will find guidance and motivation to conquer their own obstacles. Her story resonates deeply, impacting everyone who reads it.

We believe it's a divine calling, guided by the Holy Spirit, that has brought this story to life. Our mission is to share her remarkable journey and inspire others to overcome adversity with faith, courage, and resilience.

Join us in celebrating the life of a woman who defied the odds and became a "beacon of hope." Your story of victory is just waiting to be written!

* * *

Nina White

This book contains the most important keys to unlocking infinite amounts of encouragement, inspiration, tenacity, and resilience. Her story accommodates the pathways for you she has carved out with the tools of life she picked up along her path. This enriching true life story will inspire you to overcome adversity in your lives.

The author of this book is my mother, Marian West Ulrich. I am her first child and daughter, Nina. I am a product of one of her many unforeseen circumstances during her younger years of life.

However, I am alive and well able (in love) to write an introduction to this book. She learned how to bounce back when her life took her to what she thought was a dead-end road. Resilience allowed her to make a u-turn and reroute to a better pathway, toward the life she desired. She has been my mentor and friend since she birthed me. Her story is absolutely moving.

This book took years to manifest because she originally intended it to be a memoir of her life to keep in the family for generations to come.

However, by request of many to make her life story public, it has now come to fruition.

My mother has a sense of humor and oftentimes when she hears others congratulate her with a compliment for something she has accomplished, she cheerfully and humbly replies, "Teamwork Makes the Dream work and without GOD I can do nothing!"

Thank you, Mom, for giving me life and for giving me a lifetime of happiness and love.

INTRODUCTION

What should have been a pleasant Sunday afternoon turned into a twenty-year nightmare. I learned from a very early age that in a matter of mere seconds, everything good can feel like it was ripped away from you. That's how I felt one afternoon when I got news that the world I thought I knew was not altogether what I believed it to be.

My dad was a loving father and in order to protect me, he kept a family secret that I will tell you about in the upcoming chapter. Those words from the bearers of bad news ripped through my heart like a tornado, leaving me with the emotion of abandonment. I didn't realize that I internalized the anger that resulted from that day. Later in life, I remember going down the freeway asking myself why I had been so angry for the past twenty years. I've learned that even the most devastating experiences in life can be the very things that help you build wings of resilience to fly high in the face of any circumstance.

If you're a woman who smiles outwardly while crying inside, and if you've faced or are still facing a struggle, you are who I had in mind when I set out to write this book. You don't need to wait until conditions are perfect to start winning, but you can start right now from where you are.

CHAPTER 1

THE RED ROSE

My little sister Beverly and I were all dressed in white, with bobby socks and patent leather shoes. Our hair was perfectly styled into two ponytails. What a glorious Sunday it was in Webster Groves, Missouri. Not a single cloud filled the sky. Beautiful fragrances of May flowers were in bloom.

The atmosphere at the Old Community Baptist Church was upbeat, positive, and full of energy. The ladies wore their finest "Sunday go-to-meeting" clothing, and the husbands wore handsome suits, ties, and hats. We definitely felt the Lord's presence in the church that day! Everyone was so beautiful in their garments, especially the children with their red roses.

My Sister Beverly and I

After such a long and beautiful service, our stomachs were growling. As we exchanged smiles, my sister and I looked forward to the delicious scents of home-cooked food that would meet us at the door when we arrived home. We expected to sit down at the big wooden table in the dining room to enjoy the delectable feast Mama had prepared for our family and friends.

The silver-haired ladies wearing white dresses came out from behind the swinging church doors. They had previously sat shoulder-to-shoulder on a designated pew in the front row of the church. "Why are the West girls wearing red roses?" whispered one lady to another.

Suddenly, she approached us and directed her comment toward me since I was the oldest. "You and your sister are not supposed to wear red roses," she scolded. "The children wearing red roses do so because their mothers are alive. Your mother is dead, and you two girls should be wearing white roses to honor her today." We were stunned. Was Mrs. W. talking to us? Or was she confused?

The emotional blow we experienced that day was unexplainable and unimaginable. Who was our "real" mother? Why hadn't our beloved parents or another family member told us instead of this heartless approach by the silver-haired lady of the "church mother board" that we only knew from a distance? On the way home, we cried hysterically over the newfound and unwelcome information that had entered our minds that day.

From that day forward, I took on a whole new demeanor of anger that lasted until I was 28 years old, when I finally let it go. I spent the next 20 years on a path trying to "find myself." Who was I? What was my purpose? Why was I here? Why was I so different from most people I knew?

Our father sat us down and told us the entire story about our dear and courageous mother. I found out that my natural mother's name was Rose Lee Harris West, a former maid and cook who was born in the south. She grew up working on a farm in Ferriday, Louisiana, where her mother and father were sharecroppers. That's where my "tallness" came from. I was consistently told by those who knew her that Rosie Lee was a very tall and beautiful woman with a lovely smile.

She and her sister, Flora, came north to find better opportunities for themselves. They found jobs and wonderful spouses. Flora married Winfield Gaylor Sr., and Rose married William P. West. Winfield and Flora had three boys, Winfield Gaylor Jr., George, and Alex, and three daughters, Elizabeth, Jane, and Ezella.

All the cousins dearly loved their Aunt Rose and said how kindly she always treated them. However, it must have been difficult for Rose to wait so patiently, as she truly wanted to be the mother of her own children. After all, Flora's children had already grown up and started their families of their own.

Shortly after suffering a miscarriage, Rose conceived again, resulting in my birth. "Marian Delores West is her name," said Rose as she proudly held me in her arms, standing next to my father at the church to dedicate their long-awaited first-born child to the Lord in the presence of the pastor, church members, friends, and relatives.

It was kind of neat growing up knowing that I had cousins old enough to be my parents and that their children were in the same age group as me. We even attended grade school together. Though forty-one and forty-two, Rose and William appeared younger, energetic and vibrant.

It was a miracle to them that I was born, and I am thankful and honored that the Lord used me to bless them in that way.

Rose Lee West was an excellent example of a Proverbs 31 wife. She was a hard worker and had one of the most beautiful singing voices.

"Rose could sing like a bird," said Aunt Georgia.

She graced the people she met with a warm smile and pleasant spirit. She loved the Lord with all her heart and adored her husband and children. She kept an immaculate home and wore her clothes very well. Rose's culinary skills were unmatched, and she enjoyed every moment spent preparing and serving her family and friends.

I was told that she practically spoiled me as an infant, always doting on her first-born baby, for whom she had prayed and waited patiently for years. More than one person has recounted how I supposedly crawled out of her arms at church one Sunday and climbed up to the pulpit where my father was! That doesn't surprise me. As far back as I can remember, I've always been a Type-A go-getter!

Well, the good Lord saw fit to shower another blessing upon William and Rose West. On a chilly November day, they brought home a loving bundle from the hospital, the greatest gift I could have ever received. When I was only 7 months old, Rose conceived again, and my dear little sister came into my life 9 months later. Although Beverly and I are 16 months apart, we often refer to ourselves as the "delayed twins." We are so close that we often think alike and say the same thing at the same time! Beverly and I have been kindred spirits since the day she was born!

Our father was one of the strongest, yet kindest, gentlemen on the planet in our eyes. He often pondered the words of Psalm 121:1-2: "I will lift up my eyes to the hills from whence cometh my help. My help cometh from the Lord which made heaven and earth."

Why, oh why, Lord, did Daddy have to say goodbye to his beloved wife, Rose? Why did she have to die when Beverly was only 7 months old and I was just 23 months old? What in the world was breast cancer? Why did it metastasize to her liver? Why, Lord, did Rose struggle for so many years to meet the man of her dreams, a godly man with whom she had the children she longed for, only to leave so soon? God, please take care of my daddy, William West, my little sister, and me. How could this nice man handle the loss of two wives in his life?

Over a decade prior to the loss of my mother, Mattie, his first wife, had fallen dead in the kitchen while frying fish, as her daughter Verla looked on. How devastating for young Verla to witness this. She called the ambulance, but it was too late. Apparently, her mother, Mattie, had suffered a fatal asthma attack. William West knew the meaning of sorrow. He had a strong faith in God. He often read, "Trust in the Lord with all your heart and lean not unto your own understanding; in all your ways acknowledge Him, and He shall direct your paths" (Proverbs 3:5-6). William had to face the insurmountable task of raising three little girls on his own.

Verla looked after our baby sister, Beverly, and me as a toddler. Aunt Sarah and Uncle Winfield, who were up in age, helped as much as they could. In fact, they even offered to raise Beverly if my father wanted them to, but Daddy said no because he wanted to keep our family together. To this day, we are so glad that he did!

Before going to school each day, Verla would rise early in the morning to comb our hair, get us dressed, and prepare us for the babysitter.

Afterward, she would eat her breakfast, grab her books, and head out the door for school.

A few years passed, and my dad began to heal emotionally. He prayed for the Lord to send him a loving wife willing to help him raise his family.

"Yes, Mr. West, we will be back home before 11:00 pm," Ken replied in a responsible tone to our father, as he and Verla were on their way to see a neighborhood movie with my cousin Alex and Verla's best friend, Mary Lee Funches.

Mary was a bright, vivacious, and attractive high school girl who was a flag twirler, a majorette, a thespian, and a high achiever in academics. She was cheerful and uplifting, which is why Verla was drawn to her. Mary had recently moved into town with her divorced single mother, Ms. Lovie Hall. Verla and Mary really enjoyed each other's company and visited frequently. It was providential that one day my father met Mary's mother, and it was love at first sight.

Mary had a dream that she would one day have little sisters. She never gave up on that dream. After her mother, Lovie, married our father, William, we all became a blended family, and Mary now had three sisters.

I was much too young to recall all the details, but as far back as I can remember, Lovie was the only mother I knew. It was during the Mother's Day celebration at our church when Beverly and I found out that we had another mother named Rose.

We were distraught and questioned our parents about why they hadn't told us sooner. They lovingly explained that they were trying to protect us from being hurt and had planned to tell us the entire story once we were old enough to handle it.

One interesting scenario happened one night when Lovie said that my actual mother, Rose, appeared to her in a dream. Rose told her in the dream that she must "discipline Marian because she is a strong-willed child and someday will be a leader. Please don't let her think that everything she does is cute because Marian will need to learn obedience and how to follow rules." The next morning, Lovie woke up and described the lady in her dream, and William told her she had described exactly how my mother looked.

My Mom, Rose Lee Harris
(next to window below the star)

MARIAN WEST ULRICH

Maternal Grandmother: Mrs. Susan Harris
I recently visited the Frogmore Plantation where she and Grandpa Harris picked cotton.

CHAPTER 2

THE MOST TIMELY AND PERFECT GIFT FROM MOTHER

As I picked up the phone to dial out, I heard a familiar voice on the other end saying, "Hello!" Suddenly, we both broke into spontaneous laughter because, once again, we had thought of each other at the exact same time. "Girl, I was just picking up the phone to call you," I exclaimed. "No wonder I didn't hear your phone ring—you had already picked up to call me!" said Beverly.

Beverly and I are blessed to enjoy a very close relationship. When I calculate the timeframe between Beverly's birth and our mother's death, it speaks volumes about Rose West's love for her children. She was so selfless, enduring the pain and agony of cancer for nine months to bring a child into the world.

After giving birth, Rose was too ill to care for little Beverly. I have thanked God and looked to heaven countless times to thank Rose for her endurance, because she brought into the world my sister, my best friend, and confidante. As the oldest, I felt responsible for protecting her, especially after our parents passed away.

Our older sisters, Mary and Verla, were like mothers to us because of the vast difference in age. Verla married Ken, and they began their family with their first-born daughter, Val. Mary married Alex and attended a school of nursing in Spokane, WA, where they were stationed in the Air Force. Later, baby Alex Gaylor Jr. was born. Beverly and I were so happy to have nieces and nephews who were just slightly younger than we were. This allowed us all to grow up together.

Growing up together, Beverly and I have shared so many wonderful memories that it would take a separate book to name them all. We've shared mutual love, respect, and admiration without strife, competition, or envy. Instead, Beverly and I have believed in teamwork, naturally encouraging and supporting each other. As young girls, we enjoyed simple pleasures like making mud pies in a drainage ditch! Beverly was daintier than me and adored her dolls, often hosting tea parties for them. Even now, she still has collector dolls in their original boxes. I, on the other hand, usually got frustrated with my dolls and pulled their hair out due to over-combing!

We used to walk to the Webster Groves Public Library, and on the way home, Beverly's arms would be loaded with books, especially Nancy Drew mysteries. She read every book she could get her hands on, while I was content with one book at a time, spending my extra time singing and practicing with harmony and improvisation.

When we were about eight and nine years old, we had a huge adventure being hospitalized together at the People's Hospital of St. Louis, MO, for simultaneous tonsillectomies. We shared beds placed side by side in the hospital room. When our father came to visit, we were thrilled to know we were going to be rewarded with huge bowls of ice cream!

Back in the day, when we shared a bedroom, Beverly found it necessary to tape a line down the center of our room because she was super neat, and I was super untidy! Beverly has always been more reserved, while I have always been more outgoing. In these ways, we are opposites, but we truly have a heart connection.

I suppose that is another reason why we have been so close; we complement one another. Over the years, we have been there for each other, encouraging and supporting each other through school, graduations, being maid of honor at each other's weddings, childbirth and child-rearing, professional careers, and more.

We have been told many times that Beverly looks like William and has a personality like Rose, while I look like Rose and have a personality like William. It seems to me that the legacy our parents instilled in us took on a life of its own as Beverly and I reached out to love, support, and protect one another, similar to how our parents would have if they had lived.

Beverly and I have always hoped to live like the Delaney sisters, who lived past 100 years old. We hope to be too old to know if the other had passed away first. We are incredibly thankful for our close and valuable relationship and have not taken this gift for granted. Many times, when we are out and about, people approach us and say, "I wish my sister and I had a relationship like you two. It is so evident that you get along so well and are like each other's best friend."

Except for the semester I went away to college, Beverly and I had never been apart. That was until 1981, when my husband Frank, our two children, and I moved to California. This was a traumatic separation for us, and we sobbed and cried for days. Back then, there were no cell phones, email, or video calls. We ran up our phone bills so high that both our husbands complained, saying it would be cheaper to get monthly plane tickets for us than to afford the phone conversations! To this day, we are extremely grateful that God placed us in each other's lives.

My Sister Beverly and I

CHAPTER 3

ONE OF THE WORLD'S BEST DADS

Our dad communicated his love for us by being there for us, offering encouragement, protection, provision, and positive expectations. He took a special interest in teaching us how to read and spell prior to kindergarten. "M-I-S-S-I-S-S-I-P-P-I," we proudly repeated to our father as he asked us how to spell the name of the company he worked for. Mississippi Valley Structural Steel Company was one of the largest employers in the region, well-known for the fabrication of steel for bridges such as the Jefferson Bridge, the Jackson Street Bridge built in 1933, and the McDonough Bridge built in 1934.

My Dad: Rev. William P. West

The Steel Company held a "Family Open House," and we were thrilled to attend! What a huge place it was! We were looking everywhere to find our dear father, who had left that morning dressed in his usual crisp white shirt, tie, dark dress pants, and dress shoes. Finally, during the tour, we were introduced to an assembly line, and there, in the midst of many other hard-working men, was our dad dressed in work overalls, performing a job of intensive labor.

"Why is that fire coming out of that hose?" I asked. "That is called a blowtorch," someone commented. "Bill West is one of the company's finest welders!" We were so inquisitive and so proud to see that our father was willing to work such a laborious job every single day to provide for us.

In addition to his work, he paid his tuition to attend classes at seminary and served on weekends as an assistant pastor. William West was a very formal man. Each day after completing his shift, he would take a shower and dress back up into his nice white shirt, dark dress slacks, and dress shoes, and come home to sit down with our family in the most presentable way, every single day. Absolutely no exceptions or excuses.

Daddy was an exemplary father toward his children, and outstanding in the way that he loved and respected others. He was a husband, father, son, brother, uncle, grandfather and friend. Growing up as children, we cherished every moment that we got to spend with him.

He listened and was not too busy or distracted if we came to seek advice or ask for help. We especially enjoyed the positive conversations, and how he would spend time reading Bible stories to us before he tucked us into our beds at night right after we said our prayers in unison. On many occasions, we would gather around the black-and-white TV set and watch shows together with him. Some of the favorites were The Lawrence Welk Show, Lassie, Bonanza, Gunsmoke, Leave it to Beaver, and The Lone Ranger.

Whenever Sundays rolled around, we would arise early in the morning and have breakfast together as a family. Afterwards, we all would get dressed in our nice clothes that were only meant to be worn on Sundays. We admired how well our father looked and carried himself. He was definitely a fastidious dresser.

I remember him as an eloquent speaker and how proud I felt whenever he spoke from the pulpit on Sundays. His behavior and mannerisms were the same at home as he displayed in public. In all the 13 years, I knew him as a peaceful and godly man. I never heard him say any unkind or slang words. He was very intentional about treating others well. It was apparent that he lived by the golden rule.

One summer evening, after walking back home from a friend's house, I approached our driveway and greeted my father, who was working under the hood of the family car. I truly admired him because he knew how to do so many things. If he didn't know something, he would study and figure it out. He did not rest on his laurels or make false promises. Nor did he give excuses for why something couldn't or shouldn't be done.

He was steady, stable, and reliable. He would say to us, "your word is your bond." If you said you would do something, you did it without excuses. What an outstanding role model he was. Later in life, I discovered that I had built up my expectations of men based on my father—assuming they would all be like him.

Many times, I close my eyes and try to remember all the lessons our father taught us while sitting around the dining room table. If I try hard enough, I can still hear his eloquent voice in my head.

CHAPTER 4

A SENSE OF COMMUNITY

We are more alike than we are different. My father used to say, "Our family is like a bouquet of flowers. We come in every hue." We loved to be seen together with our father. What a handsome man he was! Many people have said that he reminded them of a black version of Clark Gable or a modern-day Denzel Washington.

Speaking of black, it was strange for me to realize that I was born "colored," as indicated on my birth certificate. By the time I entered fifth grade, it was discovered that I was "negro." During my later high school years, I was given another label - "black." To my amazement, the title of "African-American" was bestowed upon me during the same timeframe that I earned my bachelor's and master's degrees!

Did I receive this many titles due to my changing self or the changing culture? Who was the administrator of these title changes?

During the time frame that I wrote the original manuscript for this book, I saw a movie entitled *The Help*. It was such an awesome movie that I returned to the theater to watch it again. Perhaps many of you have read the book and have seen the movie as well. My book-loving, younger sister said, "This movie truly captured and conveyed the book's message."

She said, "I truly thought the movie did the book justice. The characters were brought to life by Viola Davis and Octavia Spencer." As an afterthought, I realized and said, "WE ARE THE HELP'S CHILDREN! We are the children and grandchildren of the women from that era!"

Back in those days, if a child did something wrong, and it was observed by any adult, that child would be reprimanded, and the parents would be called as well. Air conditioners were not common, so people would sit out on their porches to cool off in the evenings, which allowed for more opportunities to interact with neighbors in conversation. It also served as an unofficial "neighborhood watch."

Our lives were so centered around the church that the members felt like family to us. We met one of our dearest friends, Brenda Catlin, in the church foyer when we were only seven and eight years old, and have remained friends throughout the years. Brenda and her brother, Harry, were excellent pianists and singers at the church. Their mother, Hattie, was a beautiful soloist, married to our pastor, Rev. William.

Mr. and Mrs. Givens and their two sons, Albert and Jerome, were just like family to us as well. Mrs. Givens' sons were born the exact years as my sister and I were born.

On Sunday mornings, we began with Sunday School at 9:30AM, followed by church service at 11:00AM. Many afternoons were filled with musical programs, dinners, and great fellowship. Beverly and I sang in the junior choir and looked forward to attending weekly practices. Mrs. Lenora Travis was the Sunday School superintendent, organizing an annual Vacation Bible School each summer that we thoroughly enjoyed. On Saturdays, Mr. Givens and his wife Celia were in charge of the committee that created some of the finest barbecue ever prepared. It was so tasty that you could never get enough of it.

Our parents encouraged us to memorize and recite lengthy Easter speeches for the annual Easter Sunday School services. As I grew older, I took on roles such as Sunday School teacher, presenter of the weekly church announcements, and assistant record keeper of financial contributions. I deeply loved The Old Community Baptist Church and its members. It was there that I found salvation, accepted Jesus Christ as my Savior, and was baptized. It was also where I learned to study the Word of God and strengthen my faith.

Growing up in the 50s and 60s in the suburban town of Webster Groves, Missouri, we actually lived in what many people considered to be a nearly perfect place. Webster Groves is a very affluent and conservative town of six square miles. During that time, it consisted of 96% white and only 4% black.

In 1966, CBS did a special documentary called *Sixteen in Webster Groves*. Charles Kuralt stated, "CBS chose Webster Groves, Missouri for a study of teenagers because it was suburban, Midwestern, and upper middle class, and it was a statistically fair representation of towns in America, with 30,000 people."

Upon driving into Webster, the signs read: "Welcome to Webster Groves, the City of Fine Homes." There was the Kiwanis Club, the Rotary Club, the Lions Club, and the Optimist Club. Some of the comments spoken in the sequel, *Webster Groves Revisited*, described the people of Webster Groves as "status seekers and social climbers."

Our family resided in North Webster - the "other" side of the tracks, opposite the affluent part of town. It was a small section of Webster Groves where the 4% "negroes" lived. Residents took the good care of their homes and exhibited pride of ownership. Each spring and summer weekend, the neighborhood dads could be seen cutting their grass with a push reel mower and trimming the hedges to keep their lawns looking nice. During the fall, entire families would participate in raking up the leaves. When wintertime came, one could look out the window and see the fathers of each family shoveling snow from their sidewalks and driveways. A few of the homes were made of brick, while the majority were frame bungalows built after WWII.

If CBS had brought their cameras over to the north side of the tracks in Webster Groves, they may not have seen sprawling estates with rolling hills. However, had they interviewed some of the "negro" families within the modest homes, they would have found many families who were headed by loving fathers and mothers who loved the LORD with all of their hearts. These were folks who were only two generations removed from slavery, who had good values, who sacrificed and worked long, hard hours to make a better life for their children.

There was a family who put all of their children through college from the savings of their small, friendly neighborhood store. In fact, their grandson, Charles Thomas, became a famous ABC News correspondent. Mr. and Mrs. Gordon, whose daughter Janice was the only North Webster student to be interviewed by Charles Kuralt, was a fine example of entrepreneurial parents, as they owned Gordon Realty Company and Lorraine Gordon's Hair Salon.

Every winter, our neighbor, Edward Works, turned the front lawn of his parent's modest home into a winter wonderland of snow sculptures. We marveled at the beautiful reindeer he created, down to the intricate details of the delicate antlers. He later became the second African American to graduate from the School of Architecture at the prestigious Washington University in St. Louis, MO. For decades, he has been a prominent member of the AIA.

Mr. Charles Fleming was another notable figure of the North Webster community. He was actually the first African-American graduate of the prestigious Washington University School of Architecture. He went on to establish a billion-dollar international company. As an investor, he also contributed to the first financial institution founded by African-Americans, called Gateway Bank.

The Jeffersons were a vibrant, growing family who lived directly next door to us. Their daughter Renee and I were in the same grade. We used to play games like jump rope, hula-hoops, and jacks for hours on the sidewalk, having so much fun!

Their parents kept an immaculate home, a well-manicured lawn, and a shiny, polished Ford vehicle. I distinctly recall when their hard-working father took a huge leap of faith and started a Trucking company. Their business grew, and soon the company's big trucks could be seen throughout the county. That family prospered over the next generations.

Despite the fact that we North Webster neighborhood children did not have the encouragement, expectations, or guidance from our counselors at Webster Groves High School, the majority of us went on to complete bachelor's, master's, and even a few doctorate degrees. We aspired to very successful careers, including:

- Physicians
- Attorneys
- Classical musicians
- Business executives
- Commissioned officers in the US Armed Forces
- Successful business owners
- Land developers
- Building contractors

...and many other highly respectable careers, including CBS National News Correspondent, Russ Mitchell, USA Olympic Gold Medalists Ivory Crockett and Tommy Turner.

The majority of the students from the neighborhood of North Webster grew up and became wonderful parents who provided well for their own children. We were not born with a "silver spoon" in our mouths. However, we knew that with God's guidance, hard work, and focus, we had to persevere and achieve the highest levels possible to have a better life than our parents had. We knew that we could not depend on any form of a handout—not even a trust fund or a college fund. Just plain, old-fashioned hard work and "sweat equity."

As I stated before, our guidance counselors did not have the highest expectations of our abilities to become successful. "You have such a nice voice." The counselor told my sister Beverly: "You should be a receptionist someday." It's a good thing Beverly didn't limit herself to that advice because she would have missed out on something greater. In fact, Beverly rose up the corporate ladder, representing one of the world's largest and most successful pharmaceutical companies. As Director of Clinical Research, she traveled internationally, and enjoyed a very successful career.

Prior to that, Beverly was the Vice President of the Missouri Chapter of the Arthritis Foundation.

We both worked hard to pay for our tuition to graduate from college—I graduated from Washington University and my sister earned her degree from St. Louis University.

The parents of North Webster were blue-collar workers and small business proprietors. Their hard work and dedication produced so many children who reached educational and career goals far beyond what they could have imagined. Most of all, their children grew up to be productive pillars of the community.

CHAPTER 5

FAMILY LESSONS AND FAMILY TIES

We lived on North Elm Avenue in a white frame house with a very nice dining room, which was always the center of gatherings for our family and friends. We even hosted Mary's wedding to her beloved husband, Alex. There were so many wonderful memories created in that dining room. Our next favorite room was the kitchen. In the mornings, we would wake up to the wonderful

Sister Mary's Wedding in Our Dining Room

aromas of hot homemade biscuits or cinnamon rolls baking in the oven, and later sit down while our dad said a blessing over the food. After our meal, we would watch as our father backed out of the garage and left for work every weekday morning.

In the evening, dad would return from work, and Bev and I would sit down at the table with our father and mother, "Lovie," and enjoy some beautifully prepared and delicious meals. Mother Lovie displayed her kindness toward us through her outstanding culinary and sewing skills. She was a true "acts of service" person.

A typical Sunday dinner consisted of beef roast, fried chicken, mixed greens, cornbread, mashed potatoes, homemade pound cake, and homemade ice cream! She cooked from scratch. (We had never heard of a boxed cake mix until we went to college). Some other childhood favorites that she prepared were yeast rolls that would melt in your mouth with fresh butter (I could eat a dozen in one sitting), German Chocolate Cake, macaroni and cheese, steak and gravy, and the list goes on!

Mother "Lovie" had an amazing gift of being able to taste a special meal at a restaurant and come home and duplicate it perfectly. She was also a very creative and talented seamstress. In one day, she could start with a piece of fabric and turn it into a masterpiece by evening. This is how she became known as one of the best-dressed ladies at our church.

She wore lovely dresses, suits, hats, gloves, and shoes, along with accessories and handbags. Our father enjoyed his wife's beautiful appearance as he accompanied her in his nice-looking suits, fedora hat, white shirt, ties, and Stacy Adams shoes. On Sundays, the four of us would pull up to the church, where Daddy was the assistant pastor, and step out of our brand-new 1958 Plymouth, just thinking about how much we enjoyed our home life!

We cherished the way our father showed special attention towards us. One day, Daddy came home from work with a big smile on his face, saying, "Marian and Beverly, I have a surprise for you. If you can guess what it is, you can ride it after dinner!" It took us about five minutes to figure out the prize: a brand-new, shiny red wagon from the Western Auto Store. The wagon was large enough for both Beverly and me to ride in.

We coasted up and down the sidewalk for days on end, enjoying endless laughter and joy.

We also loved the help and instruction he gave us. "Always speak correctly," Daddy would say as he was teaching us to read our first-grade books. "Read with expression," he would instill in us, encouraging us not to read in a monotone pitch to prevent us from sounding dull or boring. Our dad truly helped us develop a love for reading.

To this day, my sister and I are still early risers because of those formative years when we saw our Dad arise early in the morning, read his Bible and newspaper, eat breakfast, and leave for work in his crisply ironed white shirt and dark dress pants.

My Father and Mother Lovie

The dining room table served not only as a gathering place for meals but also as a focal point for learning many life lessons.

Growing up, I recall my mother frequently quoting, "Be not deceived; God is not mocked, for whatever a man soweth, that shall he also reap" (Galatians 6:7 KJV). She wanted me to understand the importance of being obedient and sowing seeds of good character to reap a harvest of blessings instead of the opposite.

My father often encouraged me to use my singing voice for the Lord and not for worldly songs. "No man can serve two masters: for either he will hate the one and love the other; or else he will hold to the one and despise the other. Ye cannot serve God and mammon" (Matthew 6:24).

To this day, I thank them both for instilling these scriptures within me. They saved me from going down some serious paths of destruction - though I took several detours during my rebellious years, as I will discuss later.

They also taught us by example and explanation the importance of having a strong work ethic and demonstrating a high standard of excellence. Our father diligently stressed that we strive to be the best in everything we do. "Get a good education to be hired by a good company and earn a good living. Someday you girls will be able to go through doors that were never possible for me," he would say, looking into our eyes with a contented smile.

As minorities and females, we knew we would have to work twice as hard to accomplish our goals because of the prejudice that existed. Due to prejudice and Jim Crow laws, our father and his siblings were not allowed a formal education beyond the eighth grade.

Our father was a remarkable person. He treated people with kindness and respect—from his mother, siblings, and in-laws to neighbors and friends. I cannot recall ever hearing him speak negatively about anyone. He was kindhearted, intelligent, generous, and a very eloquent speaker. His own mother truly adored her son "Billy," as she affectionately called him.

Daddy was enthusiastic about recalling his childhood memories. Born in 1909, he was a young man during the Great Depression and often shared his firsthand experiences, expressing gratitude for being able to provide well for his own family. He shared stories about how he and his brothers, John and Clinton, used to walk several miles to school in the cold and raise fruit on the family farm. Every weekend, they would travel downtown with their father in a wagon to St. Louis to sell the produce at the market.

Our father made it a priority to stay connected with our relatives. Sunday after church, our father would take us to visit his mother, whom we fondly called "Grandma West." She was born in the year 1868 to parents Elijah and Elizabeth Madison. Elijah Madison served in the U.S. Civil War. He was one of the first African Americans to enlist in the Union Army 68th Regiment of the U.S. Colored Troops. In 1865, Great-grandfather Elijah was promoted to Corporal. Following the Emancipation Proclamation, he became a free man who was no longer enslaved.

After her husband John died, Grandma West moved in with her oldest daughter, our aunt, Dimple Elizabeth Wagner. Although she lived to be 97, Grandma West remained sharp, astute, and youthful throughout her life. She had two living sisters, our great aunts Parthenia and Juanita, who were also sharp and energetic ladies with excellent command of social graces. They knitted the most beautiful lace handkerchiefs. Grandma tried to teach me how to knit, but I never got past knit one, purl one!

Aunt Dimple was a "high-society" lady who hosted the Women's Cheerful Club in her home. She and Uncle Dewey had a son named Carl, and a daughter named Mabel. Our cousin Mabel Wagner-Crosby had two daughters, Muriel and Sharon, and a son named Kevin.

My Aunt "Dimple" Elizabeth West Wagner

This is another example of how we had second cousins in our age group because our parents were older when we were born. We always admired our cousin Mabel and her husband, "Buck". They lived in a lovely home down the street, and we enjoyed visiting them and listening to our cousin Sharon play classical music on the piano and organ in such an excellent fashion.

Whenever we visited Aunt Dimple's home, we looked forward to receiving delicious lemon drop candy from our grandmother. Both Aunt

Dimple and Grandma West were lovely, refined, and proper ladies. Their home was filled with various china dishes, silver tea sets, and figurines arranged in intricate places. I am sure Daddy was a little concerned that we had to be very careful not to run into anything or knock over and break his dear sister's collectibles.

Several times a year, we would travel to Elmwood to visit our Uncle Cliff Madison, and his wife, Tressie, along with their daughter Jeanette. Each year, our dad would take us way out into the country to his family homestead in an area called "Gumbo," now known as the affluent communities of Chesterfield, and Wildwood, Missouri. We would have a family picnic in Babler State Park and visit relatives like Cliff and Doris Frazier and their family, who lived in a beautiful, custom-designed home with vaulted cathedral ceilings. We thought it was the most beautiful home we had ever seen!

Daddy was definitely the glue that connected all the families together. He believed it was important for us to stay in touch with our mother Rose's side of the family, so he took us to the annual Gaylor Family Reunions every Labor Day weekend. There, we would reunite with many of our cousins: Mike, Alex, George, Jane, Elizabeth, Ezella, and all of their spouses and children. It was a joyous occasion.

North Webster hosted a carnival each year. Beverly and I were thrilled that our father took us there. He bought us cotton candy, and we rode on each attraction several times! In addition to taking us, he also brought along our cousins from our mother Lovie's side of the family, Barbara and Byron.

Daddy knew that his dear wife Lovie was close to her family and missed them terribly. One day, while sitting around the dining room table, they talked about having an annual family reunion at our home every year. A few weeks later, our mother Lovie fried up a huge amount of chicken and packed several meals for my dad and cousin to take with them as they drove all the way to Dyersberg, Tennessee, to pick up Aunt Bessie, her husband Uncle Fred, Aunt Aslee, and Christine. At the time, we children did not know that during the journey, they were not allowed to eat at any restaurant due to Jim Crow laws.

Lovie's siblings and nieces grew up together and were very close. Beverly and I absolutely loved them! They were kindhearted and very encouraging to us. Bessie Taylor was the matriarch, and her daughters were Katie, Marie, Aslee, and Christine. Even though Bessie and Lovie were sisters, Bessie and Fred raised Lovie from a child because their mother died early in life. Thus, Lovie always honored Bessie as if she were her own mother.

Each one of these ladies could definitely cook! The family reunion was laden with every type of meat you can think of, exquisite homemade cakes, huge pots of greens, and the largest trays of homemade macaroni and cheese we had ever seen.

Bessie and her husband Fred had three sons: Fred Jr., Sonny, and James. These were truly happy childhood years for us. We never felt deprived for a moment and never wondered what was next.

My Grandmother, Georgia
Madison-West
(daughter of Elijah Madison)

Gravesite of Great Grandfather Elijah
Madison (Civil War Veteran)

Even though we did not live in a mansion, we felt dearly loved by our father, and all of our family. Weeks later, around the dining room table, a discussion came up about two topics that I did not fully understand as an 8-year-old: redevelopment and eminent domain.

Apparently, the city of Webster Groves had voted to put a new road right through our property! They offered my father a certain amount of money to buy him out, and we would have to move to a new neighborhood. This presented a unique set of challenges for the homeowners affected by this new road, primarily because their homes were already paid for, and the amount of money the city was offering was not enough to pay cash for a new home. Some of the citizens did not handle this too well.

One day, as we arrived home from school, there were fire trucks, police cars, and ambulances right next door at the Chappells' home. "Don't go near the garage," shouted our mom. But it was too late. Beverly looked through the crack of the Chappells' garage and could not believe what she saw.

Poor Mr. Chappell had become so distraught over the eminent domain that he committed suicide by a self-inflicted gunshot wound. It was the saddest day we had ever witnessed as such young children. What a traumatic ordeal for his dear sweet wife, Mrs. Chappell. We stood on the sidewalk crying, as Mrs. Ruby Crump, a school teacher, escorted her mother out of the house that day. This is one of the last memories I have of our residence on Elm Avenue.

We had to say goodbye to the neighborhood that we felt so comfortable in: goodbye to Douglas Elementary School and all the students and teachers we had known since kindergarten; goodbye to

Thomas Market on the corner of Elm and Ravine, where we would stop every day to buy penny candy and bubble gum on our way home from school; and goodbye to Dixon Market at the bottom of Elm and Waymire, where we felt so grown-up going there with a "shopping list" from our mother to purchase meats and other foods. The Thomases and the Dixons were such nice families, treating everyone with dignity and respect and always being very cheerful. There was so much we were going to miss about this dear neighborhood where we were born.

Fortunately, our parents found a nice little bungalow home in the neighboring town of Rock Hill, MO, which was still in the Webster Groves school district, a great priority for our parents concerning our education. We moved to a cute two-toned yellow and brown frame home with two bedrooms, one bathroom, a kitchen, and a living room on the first floor. There was a family room, dining room, washroom, and tool room in the finished basement.

What was nice about this neighborhood was that our Uncle Cab and Aunt Katie bought the home right next door to us shortly after we moved in. Additionally, Mr. and Mrs. Bazile, the parents of my best friend Renee, bought a home just four houses up the street! We discovered that our father knew several families: the Beasleys, the Givens, the Robinsons, the famous Lofties Singers, and many more nice families, all living on Madison Avenue.

Two of the most famous residents on Madison Avenue were Bill White and Lou Brock of the St. Louis Cardinals baseball team! We loved catching a glimpse of either of them and their families as we passed by their home on our way to Schall Elementary School.

The first day of school at Schall was a baffling experience! Never before had we heard names like Bowersox, Baumgartner, Carlisle, Higginbotham, and many other names of German, Italian, and Irish origins. It was a stark contrast to the familiar faces and names we had known at Douglas Elementary School, where everyone looked similar to us and had "regular" surnames like Jefferson, Johnson, and Mitchell. This marked our first experience of stepping out of our comfort zone. Beverly and I could not believe that we were one of only a few African American families in the school.

From the very first day at Schall Elementary School, we encountered friendly children who welcomed us with open arms. They were Margie Gibson, Pam Younger, Karen Griffith, and Pam Carlisle among the girls, and for the boys, there was Steve Siebert, Billy Howell, Dennis Crump, and Mike Bowersox. We were treated kindly by many students, but these names stand out in my memory as some of the first students I met.

At Schall Elementary, there were a handful of black fifth-grade students, including my dear friends Renee Bazile and Brenda Catlin, Theodore Roosevelt Bush Jr., William Bell, Kenneth Woods, and a new boy named Raymond Johnson who had recently moved into town. Every morning, my younger sister Beverly, who was in third grade at the time, walked to school with Renee and Brenda until Brenda's health began to decline.

For some unknown reason, Brenda kept falling each day as we walked to school, but soon her condition worsened to the point where she needed our help to get up. Hattie Catlin took her daughter Brenda to St. Louis Children's Hospital, where she was diagnosed with muscular dystrophy and given a grim prognosis—possibly not living beyond her twentieth birthday. However, Brenda's strong faith in God and incredibly positive attitude defied all expectations by living over four decades beyond the doctor's predictions.

One habit that Daddy had at the dining room table proved to be extremely detrimental in later years. Whenever he sat down to eat a meal, he would sprinkle such a large amount of salt on his food before even tasting it—so much salt that it looked practically like snow. Unfortunately, this high sodium intake led to hypertension and high blood pressure.

Later, it caused his heart to become enlarged and ultimately resulted in congestive heart failure. In those days, there was no such thing as a heart transplant. Beverly and I really missed our father as he spent many days away from home, hospitalized at People's Hospital in St. Louis, MO.

Our family physician, Dr. Thomas Rusan, explained the diagnosis, and the prognosis for survival was slim to none. Although it closed in 1978, People's Hospital served for more than 60 years as the only hospital that accepted African-American physicians and patients during the days of segregation. It was a small, three-story building with 75 beds, built in 1903.

On Saturday evening, November 7, 1964, Beverly and I jumped up and down with glee because our dear father had finally come home from the hospital! "Daddy, why are your feet so swollen?" We asked. His feet looked like two piglets. Despite the edema causing his feet to swell, our father's once trim and strong physique had diminished to mere skin and bones. Congestive heart failure had led to renal failure and fluid retention in all his systems.

The next day, Sunday, marked just two days before Beverly's 12th birthday. Our mother stayed home with our father while she sent us off to church with our relatives. "Goodbye, Daddy," we said in unison as we left for Sunday School that morning, hoping to see him again upon our return. It was clear he needed rest, as he struggled to breathe and appeared to be extremely weak.

After Sunday School, Beverly and I changed into our choir robes and joined the WJC Progressive Youth Choir to sing beautiful songs. Just as we were about to sit down, an usher approached and asked us to come to the church vestibule.

"You girls need to go home now," Aunt Tressie Madison said to me tearfully when we reached her. Confused, I asked why. "Your daddy has passed away, honey," she replied, tears streaming down her cheeks. Beverly and I broke down simultaneously, holding each other up as we tried to descend the stairs and get into the car with our relatives. It was the saddest day of our lives, an unbearable grief washing over us as we arrived home and cried uncontrollably. Personally, it felt as though something had been ripped out of my soul.

My sister and I entered the house, supporting each other and trying not to succumb to fear. As we entered the bedroom, we saw our father's lifeless body lying in the large cherry wood bed.

"Daddy!" I called out to him, tugging on his lifeless shoulder. "Daddy, wake up... please don't leave us, please, please," I cried out to him.

Within the hour, Mr. Yandell and Mr. Cecile Harris, of Yandell and Sons Mortuary, came and picked up our father's body, wheeling it out under a covered sheet. This was too difficult for us to bear. What are we going to do without our beloved father? He was so young, only 55 years old, and he appeared even more youthful than his actual age.

At his funeral service, the entire church was jam-packed, with standing room only, and many people were outside. As they all filed around to view the remains of our father, many people stopped, shook our hands, and offered words of comfort. We were overwhelmed yet honored to know that the community cared so much for him. People came from many miles away, some who had known him since he was a child.

Our poor grandmother, Georgia West, at 96 years old, could not bear the pain of losing her dear son, "Billy," and went into shock. Her heart was so broken that she herself died the following month. Just three years prior, Grandma West had lost her youngest son, Clinton, to heart disease. When Clinton died, it broke my father's heart, and that was the only time we had ever seen our father cry and sob so profusely. "Clint was my favorite brother. I don't know what I am going to do without Clint in my life," Daddy said as Mother Lovie tried to console him. Beverly and I cried so hard to see our dad emotionally hurt, and we could not do anything about it.

Reviews Are Gold to Authors:
Would you consider leaving a review on Amazon?

CHAPTER 6

WORKING TO EAT

The Christmas holiday of 1964 was filled with sadness and grief due to the recent losses of our beloved father and our 96-year-old grandmother. For Thanksgiving, our sister Verla and her husband Ken invited us to their home in Richmond Heights, MO. We loved being around them because they were a young family, with plenty of nieces and nephews for Beverly and me to play with. Their oldest, Valastein, was only three years younger than Beverly.

There was also Kenneth Jr., Debbie, LaResta and baby Vickie. They had a spacious and lovely home with a large backyard. Ken worked as a supervisor for Eastern Airlines, one of the major airlines at that time.

On Christmas Day, we spent time with another favorite family, whom we considered our double relatives: Alex Sr. and Mary Gaylor and their beautiful children, Alex Jr., Brenda, Craig, and baby Valerie. We were related in two ways—first, because Alex Sr.'s mother, Flora, and my mother Rose were sisters. Years after Rose's passing, my father married Mary's mother, Lovie, making us all family. In fact, we never used the term "step-sister"; we were raised as sisters. Alex Sr. became our brother-in-law and first cousin once he married Mary. Their children were our nieces and nephews, as well as second cousins.

The Gaylor family lived on Eldridge Avenue, just around the corner from us, in a tastefully decorated house that exuded warmth and cheer. When you entered, you immediately felt at home amidst the joyful decor and sounds of laughter. We were thrilled when Alex and Mary announced they would take us and their children on a summer family vacation to Wisconsin Dells. This news lifted our spirits, giving us something positive to look forward to.

As for our father's widow, Mother Lovie, times were extremely difficult for her, and it showed in her countenance daily. The shock of losing her husband, after witnessing his prolonged suffering for many months, took a heavy toll on her.

She faced the daunting task of raising two teenage girls alone. She often reminded us that while she wasn't our biological mother and hadn't given birth to us, she was committed to raising us until at least age 18. Without her decision, Beverly and I could have been orphans.

Emotionally, psychologically, and financially, times were tough for her. Looking back, it's striking how we were at opposite ends of the hormonal spectrum: Mother Lovie was navigating menopause, while Beverly and I were squarely in the throes of puberty. This inevitably led to conflicts and yelling matches, as all three of us rode an emotional roller as we continued to grieve the loss of our father.

I deeply admire Mother Lovie's determination not to rely on welfare. She used her talents as a seamstress, crafting dresses, coats, and other garments for people in town. Her culinary skills also came to the fore as she baked delicious cakes, pies, and other recipes. Additionally, she started a small laundry service, specializing in ironing shirts for wealthy families across Webster Groves. I recall how Mrs. Smith would drop off her husband's shirts on Mondays and eagerly retrieve them on Wednesdays, marveling at how pleased her husband was with Mother Lovie's meticulous ironing, far surpassing any previous laundry service.

Word of mouth is the best form of advertising, and within a few months, Mother Lovie was earning a good living. Dr. Benjamin Davis DDS, a neighbor of our family physician Dr. Rusan, hired Mother Lovie as both a caterer and maid. This opportunity elevated her self-esteem, especially since she was working for two successful African-American families.

The wives of these families adored Mother Lovie and were deeply appreciative of her impeccable service. They marveled at her ability to prepare any dish they requested and admired her elegance and grace when hosting large gatherings. Seeing Mother Lovie succeed with her talents was a blessing for us, as it diverted her mind from the loss of our father. We were grateful to see her return home from a job she loved, knowing her employers valued her skills.

Before long, Mother Lovie's income allowed her to purchase a brand new family car. This achievement taught us an invaluable lesson about not settling for less than our best. Reflecting on those days, I am thankful for the culinary and homemaking skills I acquired. These skills have proven essential in raising my own daughters, passing down this invaluable knowledge that is often overlooked today.

I admit, as a child, I didn't appreciate Mother Lovie's insistence that I master tasks like cutting up a whole chicken perfectly. Through tears and frustration, I eventually learned these skills well. Today, many neighbors and friends have enjoyed the fried chicken I prepare, some even suggesting I turn it into a business. Their compliments affirm that Mother Lovie's recipes are timeless.

Presently, I'm experimenting with techniques to reduce cholesterol, fat, and calories in her fried chicken recipe while preserving its outstanding flavor and non-greasy texture. I cherish preparing fried chicken the old-fashioned way in a skillet. Once a year, I fry a large batch in a commercial fryer and serve it to friends and neighbors. On one occasion, I served over 100 pieces, delighting guests who devoured it as quickly as I cooked it. Thanks to Mother Lovie, this tradition continues to bring joy and connection to our community.

During the summer when I turned 14 years old, my Aunt Sarah recommended me for a babysitting job, and I started working for a family in Webster Groves. I saved up the money from my part-time babysitting job to pay for my school supplies and some of my clothes. In addition to this job, I also worked one day per week for my Aunt Katie and Uncle Cab, cleaning their house and ironing his uniforms.

If any of you ever watched the Andy Griffith show, those are the type of uniforms that Uncle Cab wore back in the day. In those days, there was no permanent press, steam iron, spray starch, or Magic Sizing. The uniforms would be very stiff from being rinsed in liquid starch. I would take a bottle of water with a sprinkler top and carefully dampen the shirts and pants, then roll them up into a towel.

Afterward, I would meticulously iron the shirts and pants just like Mother Lovie taught me. Those uniforms were ironed perfectly, as if they were done by a professional laundry! I took pride and joy in being able to do this service for my aunt and uncle because they worked extremely hard Monday through Friday.

Aunt Katie worked at the hospital as a food service worker, and Uncle Cab worked for the Webster Groves School district as a custodian. I can bet his uniforms looked sharp! They always encouraged me and told me what a good job I did for them. The money they paid me was a tremendous help for a young girl like I was.

As I mentioned previously at the beginning of this book, the CBS documentary "Sixteen in Webster Groves" was being presented to the country in 1966. At that time, I was only 14 and a student at Steger Jr. High School, which in those days provided seventh, eighth, and ninth-grade education. During the spring of my ninth-grade year, one of my teachers recommended that I try out for the Webster Groves High School A cappella Choir. After school, my dear friend Renee Bazile and I were walking home together when she informed me that she, too, was recommended to try out for the choir!

Renee and I were ecstatic because we had been singing together for several years, starting with school talent shows. Back in 1964, we formed a group called "The Flirtations" that lasted all the way through high school. We sang several songs by the Supremes such as "Stop in the Name of Love" and "Come See About Me," and we also sang "Dancing in the Street" by Martha and The Vandellas.

The group originally included Rita Brame, Renee and me in junior high, with Jackie Farewell and Anna Marie Evans. During high school, Valerie Walker and Oneida Rhodes joined us for songs like "There's A Place For Us" and many others. We loved the joy of singing. When I sang the lead part on those songs, I always pretended to be Diana Ross or

Martha and The Vandellas because it was the only way I did not feel overcome with stage fright!

Much to our dismay, Renee and I were somewhat discouraged when some of our friends reminded us of the information regarding the A Cappella Choir that was featured in the "Sixteen in Webster Groves" documentary broadcast nationwide. "There are NO Negroes in the Webster Groves High School A Cappella Choir," stated Charles Kuralt as the cameras moved across showing footage of the choir singing in perfect six-part harmony. "This is a great country, so let's shout it clear and loud. Take a look at your history book and you'll see why we should be proud!" The choir's accomplished director, Miss Ester Replogle, stood before the choir with joy and confidence, directing them through the song.

Up until this point, Renee and I had sung in our church choirs. Back in our Douglas School days, we observed how diligently Mrs. Laura Bell Turner and Mr. Walter Lathan, two outstanding musicians and teachers, poured their hearts and souls into the students at the all-Negro segregated Douglas Elementary School. They were absolute musical perfectionists who commanded a high standard of excellence in the performances and conduct of their students.

Several people indicated to me that Renee and I should not waste our time to even try out for the Webster Groves A Capella choir because several other students of our race had tried before and always had been rejected by Ester Replogle, no matter how excellent their voices were!

They said that never before in the history of the Webster Groves High School had there been any negro students in that choir and that Renee or I nor any other student did not stand a chance. Of course, it was intimidating to hear this and I was shaking like leaves of a tree on a windy day on the way to the music room of the Steger Jr. High School to tryout before Miss Ester Replogle that day!

I prayed heavily to the Lord and took a deep breath and entered the room where Miss Replogle was seated at the piano. A week later, I thanked the Lord God Almighty for answering my prayers because the names of Renee Bazile and Marian West appeared on the list of students who were chosen to participate in the Webster Groves High School A Capella Choir! All of my family was so happy and I was somewhat saddened that my father had not lived to see this happen.

Photo of WGHS Acapella Choir from 1969 Yearbook

Through our involvement in the A Cappella Choir, we learned to sing many genres of music and excelled in performances such as "West Side Story," "Oklahoma!," "The Mikado," and other Broadway musicals.

Ester Replogle, affectionately known as "Miss Rep," dedicated her life to educating and directing students in the performing arts. She instilled in us a deep appreciation for classical composers throughout history. One of my favorites was Handel, who composed "The Messiah." I particularly enjoyed singing the "Hallelujah Chorus" in concerts, graduations, and baccalaureate services.

One of the greatest honors was singing with the St. Louis Symphony Orchestra under the direction of Elizo De Cavallo. During the Christmas production, I even had a small solo, which boosted my confidence and affirmed that my musical ability mattered more than the color of my skin.

Above all, the choir taught me that we students were more alike than different. I cannot recall a single derogatory comment or incident towards Renee and me. All the choir members treated us with kindness and respect. We even became close friends with some, like Janet Carter.

Janet, one of the school's most popular girls and a cheerleader, along with her best friend Candace, who had blonde hair, blue eyes, and outgoing personalities, were very welcoming toward me. Visiting Janet's home, I admired her family's graciousness and asked about her father's profession. "He's a CPA," Janet explained, which left me impressed. This encounter planted a seed of ambition in me.

Candace unknowingly inspired me further when she arrived at school one day in her candy apple red Mustang fastback with white leather interior, a gift from her father for her birthday. Seeing that car sparked a dream in me to own a Mustang one day. Although I lacked the means then, I realized that with hard work and saving, my dream could become a reality someday.

To my amazement, Janet had a vinyl record collection that was very similar to mine at home! She played several selections by the Supremes and the Temptations. I'll never forget how Janet made me laugh so hard one day when she asked me how I knew all the words to every single song on the vinyl albums. I replied, "Why Janet, don't you know the words too?" She responded, "No, Marian, I just love the music and the beat!"

Later that spring, Janet visited my home for a school project. Thanks to Mother Lovie's meticulous housekeeping and gracious hospitality skills, I never felt embarrassed to invite friends over. Despite our small house, it was always clean and organized. We were taught to clean from a young age, and our rooms had to be spotless. I once got reprimanded for leaving my shoes under the bed instead of in the closet!

We thoroughly enjoyed Janet's visit, which lasted from afternoon into the evening. She had a pleasant attitude and genuinely accepted people for who they were. Janet also shared with me that she was a Christian and involved in an organization called Young Life, which I hadn't heard about before. Reflecting on my yearbook, I found a handwritten note from Janet on page 75:

"Marian, this has been such a rewarding year for me getting to know you better. Thank you for helping me with spring sports. You are one of the most talented people I know, and you're just altogether great! I hope our friendship continues to grow next year as it has this year. Good luck always, Love, Janet Carter."

Without the involvement of the WGHS Acapella Choir, friendships like ours would never have blossomed.

CHAPTER 7
WORKING AT A FIVE AND DIME STORE

I matured quickly in the months leading up to my 16th birthday and it occurred to me that I could apply for a "real" job. I applied at the Crestwood Shopping Plaza to work as a cashier at JJ Newberry's–a five and dime store! I was thrilled when I got the job because it meant I could wear one of those light blue smocks and a name tag.

I was fortunate to carpool to work with a neighbor, May Lofties, who was a senior cashier at the same store. On my first day, I was greeted by a familiar face from school, Paula Johnson! Paula had been optimistic and friendly, and knowing that she was starting work the same day made me feel more at ease. We were both the "new kids on the block," so to speak.

This job suited me perfectly because I enjoyed interacting with people, helping them with their purchases, and counting back change into their hands. In those days, there were no digital cash registers—just old-fashioned manual ones. It was essential to know how to count change because those registers didn't tell you how much to give back to the customer. Additionally, all clocks were round with two hands and 12 numbers, and time cards were cardboard requiring actual sign-ins.

Working at J. Newberry's was a wonderful experience. I loved earning a paycheck with my name, Marian West, printed on it. Opening my own bank account at Webster Groves Bank & Trust made me feel very independent. I made sure to set aside 10% for tithes and helped our mother with the bills. The rest was mine—all mine!

On my way home from the bank, I passed Lockwood Avenue and noticed a van driven by an African-American man. The sign on the van read "Jimmy Williams Maid and Janitor Service." I quickly wrote down the telephone number and tucked it into my purse. The following week, I called and spoke with the receptionist/secretary, who scheduled an interview with Mr. Williams himself.

The next week, I took a shortcut across the expansive lawn adjacent to the Edgewood Children's Orphanage. As I walked, I thanked the Lord that neither my sister Beverly nor I had ever needed to live there, as both our natural parents were now in heaven. I prayed for success in my interview with Jimmy Williams Janitor and Maid Service. The shortcut shaved about 15 minutes off my trip, allowing me to arrive early and gather my thoughts.

"Miss West, Mr. Williams will see you now," said the receptionist. To my surprise, the man who greeted me with a firm handshake and friendly smile was Mr. Jimmy Williams himself—the same man I had seen driving the van a few days earlier. It brought me joy to see that the owner of the business was a black man. What a wonderful role model, I thought!

Mr. Williams was a very astute and professional businessman with a calm and caring demeanor. He carefully reviewed my application and asked several questions during the interview. He thanked me for coming, and a few days later, his secretary called to ask when I could start working.

I was thrilled because now I could earn $13.50 per day! During the summer and into the fall after school started, I would work at least two Saturdays each month. I also referred my friend Jackie to the company, and she got hired too. It was great because now we could ride together in the big van out west to the very affluent town of Ladue, MO in the mornings and evenings.

It was quite a coincidence that Jackie worked for the Levinson family and I worked for the Miller family, who happened to be best friends living in adjacent neighborhoods. Both families were extremely kind and introduced us to Jewish traditions and new foods, including a delicious liver pâté. They attended a place of worship called a Temple, and they had a beautiful Weimaraner dog as a family pet.

My responsibilities included managing the kitchen for the children's meals and cleaning up afterward, along with other chores to give Mrs. Miller a break from her lively family. Working for this lovely family expanded my dreams for the future, imagining what it would be like to have such a lifestyle.

The summer passed quickly, and the job ended just before the school year began. I often think about the Miller family and wonder how they are doing. They probably don't realize the positive impact they made on my life.

Mr. Williams later informed me that he had received very positive feedback on my work ethic, and the Miller family had rated my performance as excellent. He assured me that his secretary would contact me about any future part-time Saturday job openings.

Weeks later, I received a new assignment to work Saturdays for a young couple right there in Webster Groves named Paul and Judy Brackens.

I was thrilled to be able to walk the miles to work there every other Saturday for the Brackens! They had a huge and friendly German Shepherd as their family pet. At that time, they didn't have any children yet. My job was to clean their home every other week. Paul and Judy Brackens have no idea how much their encouragement helped expand my thinking process to realize that I could have a great life someday.

Paul was an attorney with an office in Clayton, MO. He had recently graduated from Washington University in St. Louis, one of the most prestigious schools in the country. Judy, also a Washington University graduate, worked at AT&T headquarters in downtown St. Louis as a computer programmer. Little did I know then that someday in the future, the Lord would pave the way for me to graduate from Washington University also and pursue a professional career at AT&T. Praise God!

From the Brackens, I learned how important it is to see yourself as you CAN be, not just focus on where you are. Someday, if possible, I would like to meet them and thank them for their encouraging influence on my young mind, showing me the possibilities that life can offer.

CHAPTER 8

LOOKING FOR LOVE IN THE WRONG PLACES

It is crucial for a daughter to receive love and guidance from her father, especially during her formative years and even more so as she enters adolescence. Growing up in a household where she witnesses the qualities of a good man and how well he treats his wife and children provides a valuable model for the qualities she should seek in a future spouse.

Numerous studies have shown that if a girl lacks approval, love, and attention from her father, she may seek these elsewhere. Without a positive paternal influence, many girls are at higher risk for serious social and psychological issues, including insecurity, and feelings of being unloved and unwanted. They may struggle without clear boundaries. During my teenage years in high school, I felt awkward, lonely, and unattractive, desperately needing affirmation that I was okay.

Losing my father was emotionally devastating. Why did he have to die and leave us? As a young child who lost her mother just a month before my second birthday, I never truly knew her. Hearing others praise her kindness and love for us only made me feel abandoned and left me longing for a mother's love.

Throughout high school, I dated a respectful young man named Billy, who treated me kindly and with great respect. He was well-regarded by our classmates, and his kindness and good upbringing were evident in how he treated me. Billy's family background, his involvement in sports, and his popularity among our peers made our time together enjoyable, whether riding around in his Oldsmobile Cutlass 442, going to movies, or attending school events.

During the summer before college, our steady relationship abruptly ended, leaving me heartbroken and devastated. Young love is challenging. Throughout junior high and high school, I maintained a "goody two-shoes" image, guided by the moral values instilled by my parents. After my father's death, our stepmother Lovie raised us as a single mom, prioritizing our upbringing over her personal life. She set a moral example, teaching us values such as abstaining from smoking, drinking alcohol, and using drugs, and saving our virginity for marriage. Despite this upbringing, I struggled with deepening emotional pain, leading me down a path of promiscuity to numb my feelings of abandonment.

In my despair, I sought to fill a void that seemed to grow deeper, despite my efforts. The voices in my head reinforced feelings of being unloved and unimportant. Despite their absence being beyond their control, I felt abandoned by my parents, who both passed away when I needed their love and guidance the most.

The question "Who cares about me, anyway?" echoed in my mind, with the answer "No one. So what?" The attempt to fill that void was futile, like trying to pour water into a sieve—whatever I poured in just drained away.

As adolescence set in, I began to feel a strong attraction to many boys. I entered a phase of styling my hair, wearing makeup, and dressing in appealing clothing. I hung out with other teenage girls who, like me, lacked the protective presence of a father at home due to divorce, separation, or being raised by a single mother.

When my father was alive, he often reminded me of Matthew 6:24: "No one can serve two masters: for either he will hate the one, and love the other; or else he will hold to the one, and despise the other. You cannot serve God and mammon."

In a defiant tone, I once replied, "But Daddy, I want to grow up and be a singer like Diana Ross of the Supremes! I even made it to the school talent show, and everyone liked our singing group. Why aren't you proud of me for being the lead singer, Daddy?"

"Marian, when you sing solos during Sunday morning church services, recite your Easter speeches by memory, or read the Sunday morning announcements, you are doing those things for the Lord, and that's when I am proud of you," my father explained.

Reflecting on this exchange with my father, I now wish I had heeded his teachings more and stayed on the right path.

After breaking up with "Mr. Right," whom I had thought I would marry, I couldn't wait to leave town and go away to college.

That summer before college, I interned at a telecommunications company in downtown St. Louis, Missouri. This internship was pivotal for building my future career. It was an exciting daily adventure traveling into the big city with my childhood friend Renee to 1010 Pine, an iconic building that housed the Southwestern Bell headquarters for the Southwestern region.

By then, I had saved enough money to buy my dream car, a 1966 light blue Ford Mustang. Ever since seeing my classmate drive her beautiful Mustang so many years before, owning one became my goal. I felt like one of the coolest girls around, and nothing could convince me otherwise!

The only thing I didn't look forward to about going away to college was leaving my little sister Beverly behind. We were incredibly close and always each other's anchor.

In the fall, my friend Jackie Farwell, whom I had known since grade school, and I were so excited for the four-hour journey to arrive in time for freshman orientation at Southeast Missouri State University in Cape Girardeau, Missouri. The campus, also known as "Cape State," buzzed with youthful energy, drawing students from all over Missouri—some friendly, others more reserved.

Wow! Look at all those football players! Whew! I had to keep my composure, though I felt a mix of shyness, excitement, and self-assuredness.

Once dorm roommates were assigned, we met students from rival schools like Kirkwood High School and others. For some reason, I felt a sudden need to compete with these girls, who I perceived as prettier, better dressed, and more popular than me.

It dawned on me that my singing talent might be my ticket to standing out. Within weeks, I auditioned for the university talent show, singing "Alfie" by Burt Bacharach, made famous by Dionne Warwick. It was a hit! They liked me! I was invited to perform in the show, and the announcer introduced me as "Cape State's Dionne Warwick—Miss Marian West!" The applause was exhilarating, and it felt amazing to be appreciated for my talent.

Little did I know, this marked the start of a journey down the wrong path—a path my father had warned me about when he was alive.

Being accepted into the "cool crowd" felt like a victory. However, I couldn't handle the peer pressure and situations that came with it. Despite being smart, I was really naïve! Everyone in our group claimed to have lost their virginity in high school, and I was labeled "frigid" because I was still a virgin. 1 Thessalonians 5:22 advises to "abstain from all appearance of evil." Reflecting on and living by this verse could have steered me away from the downward spiral that followed.

Mother Lovie often quoted Galatians 6:7, "Be not deceived; God is not mocked: for whatever a man soweth, that shall he also reap." Boy, did I get tired of hearing her repeat that verse all the time. By now, I was starting to become rebellious.

An opportunity arose to attend a party downtown, and I eagerly prepared to look my best because a group of my girlfriends would be picking me up to go together. I was so nervous that my knees were shaking. I wore a beautiful black and white summer-printed A-line dress, my hair pulled back and adorned with a lovely coordinating hair bow. I had practiced walking with a book on my head so many times that I could glide into a room and make a very elegant entrance.

"Would you like to dance?" said the most absolutely handsome man I had ever seen in my entire life! He was tall, tanned, polite, and seemed very patient. "Marian, go ahead and dance with him!" exclaimed my friend with glee. I danced with him again and again that evening. During our time together, I learned that he had just returned from Vietnam after serving six years in the United States Marine Corps. How intriguing, I thought. Later that evening, he introduced me to his two cousins, who were both girls close to my age and asked for my phone number so he could reach me again.

On the way home that night, my friends and I couldn't stop talking about how impressive this young man was! "Wow, I'm so glad I came to this party with you all," I exclaimed joyfully.

The phone kept ringing off the hook. Day after day, our "love" for each other grew (or so I thought). I loved it when he showed up at our modest home, driving an even nicer car than the Chevy Belair my mother drove to work.

He asked my mom for permission to take me on a date. I was so excited! I wondered which movie he would choose. Maybe we'd go to another "cool" party like the one where we first met!

We pulled up to a dimly lit building that I'll never forget. The name that showed up in lights on the outside of the building did NOT say "movie theater."

This smooth-talking, handsome man told me he loved me and that I needed to prove my love by coming into this dreary place and giving myself completely to him. Foolishly, I thought, "I'm a grown woman now! I've turned nineteen, one year past legal age. Why not give myself to this wonderful man who says he loves me, wants to spend his life with me? I longed for a good man I could depend on, to build a beautiful family and an ideal life together, like my father had with my mother Rose or my stepmother Lovie.

"Oh Lord, what have I gotten myself into?" I thought. "This is nothing like I imagined." There was no honeymoon suite, no glorious church wedding surrounded by loved-ones throwing rice as we left. Suddenly, I realized my mistake, but I couldn't turn back now. Remembering advice from my experienced friends, "always make sure he uses protection or withdraws so you won't get pregnant."

During the summer, I was highly recommended to work for one of the wealthiest and most prominent families in Missouri. My job was to work as a weekend governess for their youngest son, about three years old. "What a beautiful estate," I thought as I pulled up in my light blue 1966 Mustang. The main house looked like a castle, reminiscent of those in the English countryside. The housekeeper introduced me to Mrs. M, who exuded extreme wealth and refinement. She interviewed me politely, and I could tell we connected well.

After the interview, Mrs. M led me to the west wing and showed me my own personal bedroom and bathroom where I would stay every weekend while caring for her child. It was astonishing to learn they had three children—two boys and a girl—and employed separate governesses for each child during both weekdays and weekends. One key instruction I received was that the children should never eat together at the same table, and when I took the youngest on outings, I had to avoid running into his siblings. I recall during a July 4th parade, seeing the father with one of the other children from a distance, and I had to ensure the young boy didn't spot them in the crowd.

There have been many days when I've prayed and wondered how these children turned out in life. I felt sorry for them because they seemed to lack the family interaction that I was fortunate to have experienced.

Despite our family not being rich in material wealth, the love we shared and the time our parents spent with us created priceless memories.

This early observation taught me a powerful lesson: the best way to show children love is by spending quality time with them, not delegating their care daily to governesses. Undoubtedly, they may have been sent off to boarding school once they reached a certain age.

Approximately six weeks after starting my job as a governess, I began feeling as though I had come down with the stomach flu. I felt tired and queasy every single day that week.

"Is that you I hear throwing up in the bathroom? You sound like a pregnant woman to me," said Mother Lovie. Fear gripped my heart. "It's impossible to get pregnant the first time you're with a boy," I whispered as an effort to reassure myself.

If Mother Lovie knew I had truly been with a boy, she would have been so disappointed. And if my dear father were still alive, he would have been furious! In fact, if he were alive, maybe it wouldn't have happened. Losing his guidance and dealing with the emotional pain daily was unbearable. I didn't turn to drugs, drinking, or wild parties, but raging adolescent hormones clouded my judgment. I was losing control of the morals I had learned from the Bible and the lessons my parents taught me were disregarded.

The Bible says, "Flee from sexual immorality. All other sins a person commits are outside the body, but whoever sins sexually, sins against their own body" (1 Corinthians 6:18). Unfortunately, during this period of my life, I defied God's word, and verses like this fell on deaf ears.

For this, I am not proud. I share this with you so that you may realize the extent of God's grace toward you in areas of sin where you may be entangled. There are many forms of sin—gossip, lies, fornication, abortion, adultery, infidelity, unclean thoughts, slander, jealousy. Thank God for His mercy, His grace, and His forgiveness!

This is probably just the flu, I thought. However, weeks later, my normal menstrual period, which always occurred every 28 days like clockwork, DID NOT HAPPEN!

The days and weeks that followed were among the most emotionally testing I had ever experienced in my life up to that point.

"What's new with you, kid?" "What have you got coming?" Mrs. Jackson, a jovial and kindhearted lady, asked with a big smile as she walked down the church steps one Sunday morning.

"Oh, Lord," I thought to myself, "How did Mrs. Jackson find out? I'm still as tall and skinny as ever. I'm not showing... How did she know that my lab results were positive?"

Reflecting on my recent visit to the doctor's office, that confirmed my pregnancy, I felt like I had let my parents down and suddenly, I started sobbing uncontrollably. "I WANTED TO GO TO COLLEGE!!! NOW WHAT AM I GOING TO DO???"

CHAPTER 9

A CROSSROADS AND A CHOICE TO MAKE

As the gravity of my situation sank in, I realized that I had a very important choice to make. Would I continue with the pregnancy, risking criticism and disappointment from my family and friends? Would I possibly ruin my chances of ever attending and finishing college? Would I risk missing my lifelong dream of becoming successful? I was only 19 years old, and pregnancy was definitely not an ideal task on a to-do list.

On the other hand, during the 1960s and 1970s an alternate plan became the topic of heated debate–abortion. Many in the culture were expressing the "right" that women possessed to "choose" what was best for them. If pregnancy came at an inopportune time, steps could be taken to terminate the whole thing.

As for me, I could not bear the thought of ending the life that was inside of me. Bible verses such as, "Before I formed you in the womb I knew you.." (Jeremiah 1:5), as well as, "And we know that all things work together for good to them that love God, to them who are the called according to his purpose," (Romans 8:28) rang clear in my heart.

Besides that, I knew that my lapse in good judgment had already saddened the heart of God. I did not want to compound matters by taking the life of my precious child.

I decided to trust the LORD and keep my baby. I knew that the LORD would provide, and that HE would help us through this tough season.

The Bible states that "If we confess our sins He is faithful and just to forgive our sins and cleanse us from all unrighteousness" (1 JOHN 1:9). If someone had told me that I would be confessing my sins to potentially thousands or even millions of people, I would never have believed it. Yet, here I am, sharing and exposing my mistakes and shortcomings to help you understand that many people, like myself, have faced heartbreaking trials, failed miserably, and deeply disappointed God.

Do I believe I deserve God's forgiveness?

No, I do not.

But I am eternally grateful that God Himself lifted me out of the lonely, destructive path and restored my heart, self-respect, and deepened my love and relationship with Christ.

Reflecting on my life, I shudder at the reckless mistakes driven by a rebellious spirit of pride and bitterness, which was rage turned inward. I vividly recall sitting on the floor, crying, "I just want to find myself!"

Looking back, the solution is clear. If only I had changed those words to say, "God, I just want to find YOU!" This plea would have shown submission to God's authority and surrendered my strong-willed attitude to Him.

Despite our failings, God's love, unwavering grace, and mercy have given us the greatest gift: His own Son, Jesus Christ. He is the One who came to earth sinless, died on the cross, and bore excruciating pain as a ransom and sacrifice for all our sins. Whether your sins involve abortion, gossip, or gluttony, sin is sin in the eyes of the Lord. However, there is no sin too great for God to forgive when we accept and believe in Jesus Christ as our Savior. He completely wiped the slate clean for me, and He will do the same for you.

It would not be right, nor would I have the authority to judge anyone for their personal beliefs and actions; that responsibility belongs to God alone. Nevertheless, I feel compelled to explain my perspective as I was faced with this decision at a young and tender age. Now I stand on the other side looking back. Although things were difficult, I do not regret for one moment having the opportunity to raise my daughter and watch her grow into the beautiful woman she is today.

CHAPTER 10

WHAT WILL I NAME HER?

It was the day before Valentine's Day, and I was singing along with my friend Brenda and her mother Hattie to a special song titled "Keys to the Kingdom". Brenda played the music beautifully, blending her mother's melodious soprano with my alto voice, while other choir members joined in the chorus in perfect harmony.

By now, I couldn't see my feet due to my eighth-month pregnancy belly. As I sang the second verse, I felt the baby kick strongly, as if she understood the song! "When that baby comes, we will call her Keys, just like keys to the kingdom!" said Mrs. Hattie Catlin.

Later that evening, the father of my child came over with a large red heart-shaped box filled with Valentine chocolates. He brought both sweet chocolates and bittersweet news. The good news: he wished me a happy Valentine's Day. The bittersweet news: he revealed he was expecting another child with someone else and had decided to marry her. I was devastated.

What about our child? I asked. What about us? I cried. He explained he couldn't see himself marrying me because my mother was too strict, and he felt more compatible with the other girl and her family.

After he left, I cried and sobbed alone. Finally, I opened the box of chocolates, taking a bite, then another, when suddenly I felt a pain unlike any before. Oh God! It's too soon for my baby. My due date isn't until March! Shortly after, Mother Lovie arrived home and realized I was in labor.

It was an extremely cold winter's night, and the snow was piled high upon the sides of the highway. The drive seemed like it took forever to finally arrive at the hospital. The physical pain was absolutely unbearable as I opened the car door, climbed out of the backseat, and slowly walked toward the hospital's ER entrance doors, left alone to fend for myself and my soon-to-be-born child. There was no person to hold my hand; there was no person to calm my fears. Tears were streaming down my face due to a broken heart. At this point, I felt so unloved, rejected and mistreated.

My ob/gyn had reserved a place for me and suddenly a group of kind-hearted and caring nurses came and immediately wheeled me to the Labor and Delivery room. It was the kindness of those nurses who consoled me and I will always remember how they pulled me through such emotional pain that night.

At 4:03 am on Valentine's Day, my labor pains ceased with the arrival of the most beautiful earth angel, my daughter Nina! The nurse announced that she was 4 weeks premature and needed to be kept in an incubator due to her birth weight of less than 5 pounds. It was overwhelming. The last 48 hours had been a whirlwind.

I called home to tell Mother Lovie and my sister Beverly about my baby girl! We thought I was having a boy and hadn't picked out a girl's name. Then I remembered babysitting Mrs. Shirley Woolfolk's daughters,

Venice and Vickie, who had a friend named Nina. I loved the name Nina instantly, and from that moment, she became Nina to us all.

Valentine's Day was the perfect day for Nina to be born because she has been a sweetheart her entire life. Her birth was truly a blessing from God! I was overjoyed to return to the hospital on a cold winter's day, bundle her up, and take her home with me!

"Thank You, Lord, for this wonderful child, and please help me be a good mother."

The Bible says, "Arise, take up thy bed and walk," (John 5:8) and that is exactly what I intended to do.

Reviews Are Gold to Authors:
Would you consider leaving a review on Amazon?

CHAPTER 11

THE PROMISE: HOW I AVOIDED THE WELFARE AID TRAP

What a glorious day it was when we returned to the hospital to bring Nina home! Placing her in the white bassinet lined with yellow blankets and bedding brought us such joy.

Like any newborn, Nina began demanding her formula at just two weeks old with a loud cry. "That baby has a good set of lungs," said her proud Aunt Beverly, and we laughed together. Both of us marveled at how tiny she was, almost swallowed up by her newborn clothing. With round-the-clock feedings of Enfamil Formula, Nina quickly gained weight and became a healthy, thriving baby.

Thankfully, Nina's father and his family provided all of her formula, diapers, and other necessities, as my savings were about to run out. Mother Lovie asked me a crucial question: "Marian, how do you plan to support Baby Nina?"

I walked over to the bassinet, gently lifted Nina into my arms, and vowed from my heart,

"You are such a precious and beautiful baby girl. You didn't ask to come into this world, but God sent you through me. I accept the responsibility to raise you right, with God's help. From now on, I will take excellent care of you. You will always receive my unconditional love, have plenty to eat, and wear beautiful clothes. I will complete my college education, earn a B.S. and MBA, degree and secure a well-paying career to provide for you.

"We will have a house, and you will have your own room. You will attend excellent schools, and I will save for your college education. At 16, you'll have a car. Above all, I will raise you in the ways of the Lord, teaching you values with eternal significance. Someday, I will marry, and you WILL have a father! But until then, I will be your mother and your father."

This promise was spoken to Nina when she was just three weeks old. I was determined that we would not end up as statistics depending on handouts to survive.

By the grace of God and years of hard work, trials, and struggles, that promise came true. Motherhood came earlier than planned, but it led me down a challenging path that ultimately benefited both my child and me. I was determined not to let my daughter down; I had spoken these commitments, and I would not backtrack. There is power in spoken words.

Remembering my father's teaching that, "Your word is your bond," I knew that I could not make a promise and not follow through.

Me holding baby Nina

When Nina turned eight weeks old, I got into my light blue 1966 Mustang and drove over to South St. Louis. I applied for a job as a food service worker at a convalescent home. After filling out the application, there was an immediate interview, and I was hired on the spot! This made me feel so happy because I would now have a steady income to provide for my daughter's needs.

After working there for about 2 months, one of my coworkers found out that I had a baby at home. She befriended me and we started taking our lunch hour together. We really enjoyed the food there! Ms. Pearl, the head cook, was outstanding, and she always gave us large helpings. She used to say, "Child, you need to eat more to put some meat on your bones!" During the morning breaks, Ms. Pearl would always give me an extra helping of hot cereal in her attempt to fatten me up!

One day, another young woman who was also 20 years of age like me asked whether I received checks from ADC? Not wanting to sound dumb or uninformed, I reluctantly admitted that I did not know what that stood for. "Aid to Dependent Children," she replied. She explained to me that she was receiving a monthly government check for her son and also additional benefits as well. I told her that I did not need ADC because I was trusting God to help me complete my education, have a high-paying professional career in business, and make a lot of money.

Of course, she laughed at me and shrugged her shoulders in a fashion that indicated she did not hear the response that she was expecting from a person whom she assumed was in a very desperate situation in life. I thought back to the example of my parents. My father always had an excellent work ethic.

I was told that Rose, my biological mother, was a very hard worker. I observed how Mother Lovie, after the death of my father, turned her culinary and meticulous housekeeping skills into resources to earn an income through a laundry business, a caterer, a dressmaker, and a maid. As far as the education was concerned, I read time and time again the newspaper clipping of my cousin Joyce West, who earned her Master's Degree from Loyola University in Chicago.

Joyce was several years my senior and was a true role model for me. Because of the age gap we did not grown up together. However, I was so very proud of Joyce from a distance. Her example actually gave me a roadmap to follow. It made me realize that if Joyce could do it, so could I. Since then, Joyce completed her PhD. and went on to become a professor at Boson University for many years.

After praying and seeking God's direction, I decided to step out on faith to become a more productive person who set goals and put forth the effort to achieve them. This path strengthened me along the way and provided personal growth by requiring me to overcome obstacles and roadblocks.

There is an old saying that you may have heard before that bears repeating... "You can give a man a fish and feed him for a day. Or, you can teach him how to fish and feed him for a lifetime." Had I applied for a government welfare check, that would have been only a fish for a day. I could have been tempted to become complacent and miss out on greater things. I chose to become a "fisherwoman" to learn how to be successful for a lifetime.

CHAPTER 12
JOB BY DAY UNIVERSITY BY NIGHT

Working at the convalescent home was very fulfilling. The part I enjoyed most was interacting with elderly patients, who deeply appreciated the attention since many had no visitors. While it provided a steady paycheck, I knew it wasn't my long-term career goal. On my days off, I diligently applied for positions at major companies in the area. Mother Lovie encouraged me, saying, "Marian, you're so smart! I'm sure you'll someday have multiple job offers!"

About three weeks later, faced with a dilemma, I sought my mother's advice. I had offers from the State of Missouri, as well as Western Electric (later AT&T Technologies). Initially, I leaned towards Missouri due to a higher starting salary of $414.00, but AT&T offered a more promising career path.

Driving up to 1111 Woodsmill Rd. in Ballwin, MO was exhilarating. The sprawling campus, rows of parked cars, and impeccably manicured landscape made me feel part of something great. Entering through the huge double doors, I was warmly greeted by a receptionist and escorted to the new employee orientation in the personnel department. Finally, I felt like I belonged to a professional company.

Coincidentally, my baby daughter turned six months old on my first day, and a cost-of-living raise increased my starting salary by $35.00 per month, effectively making it higher than the State of Missouri job.

I'm forever grateful for the opportunity at the Bell System, which laid the foundation for many accomplishments in my career.

In the entry-level accounting clerk department, I worked under Ned Hummer, a kind, Christian, family man with a gentle demeanor. He was the opposite of autocratic. He fostered a positive work environment and brought out the best in people. My close friends and coworkers, Sandy and Yvonne, and I often ate together in the cafeteria or at local restaurants. It was refreshing to be in a workplace where people took pride in their appearance and job. Our workdays lasted seven and a half hours, and I eagerly looked forward to each day.

During my first week, I met several coworkers including Carol, Kathy, and a young man named Earl Branch who informed me he was majoring in accounting at Washington University. "That's very impressive, Earl," I said. He explained he was part of the Bell System reimbursement plan, with AT&T covering his entire tuition.

Earl was also a veteran, studying under the GI Bill. I truly admired him for his accomplishments and determination, as did his equally productive wife, Jean, who was studying to become an RN and had recently given birth to twins.

That evening, I pondered what it would take for me to enroll at my dream school, Washington University. Until then, it had only been a dream, but now it seemed within reach.

The next day, I made an appointment to speak with Mr. Bill Wilkins, one of the few African Americans in management at the company. Mr. Wilkins was pleasant and professional, guiding me through the Employee Tuition Reimbursement Program. A few months later, I received the joyous news of my acceptance to Washington University. I was ecstatic to read the letter!

Meanwhile, Beverly and I had saved enough to rent our first apartment in University City, just a few miles from the university campus. We rented the spacious second floor of a charming two-story brick duplex. Downstairs lived the Jones family—Mr. and Mrs. Jones and their son Mark, who was Nina's age. It was a blessing because Nina and Mark got along well, and Mrs. Jones began babysitting both children, which was mutually beneficial.

Beverly, while preparing for college herself, would take Nina downstairs in the mornings on her way to school, and pick her up in the evenings while I attended classes at night.

Beverly and I regularly sat down to plan our goals together. We were determined to graduate within four years. We strategized, budgeted, and planned for our future careers. I worked full-time at AT&T from 7:00 am to 3:30 pm, allowing me to attend my first class at Washington University by 5:00 pm. With the psychology department's permission, I could also take several courses on an independent study basis, effectively managing a full-time load of 15 college units per semester.

Transferring some credits from Meramec Community College and a semester at Southeast Missouri State University put me on track to graduate with a B.S. in Psychology by May 1976. This timeline was three years later than if I had gone straight from high school, but Nina, who would be five years old by then, could be there with me at graduation, making it a special day for both of us.

I remember there were times when I had to take Nina with me to school at night when I couldn't find a babysitter. One evening, we arrived twenty minutes late for my English Literature class. The professor called me aside just after I had quietly settled into my seat, motioning for Nina to stay quiet as she colored in her book.

In a sharp tone, he looked sternly into my eyes and said, "Miss West, you consistently arrive late to my class. You disrupt the other students, and you bring your child to my class. I find this greatly annoying. However, in all my years as a professor, I have yet to encounter a student who can write so well under pressure as you. Therefore, I have no other choice but to give you an 'A' in this class!" "Oh my goodness! Thank you," I replied. I silently prayed and thanked the Lord for His blessing as I returned to my seat. The professor might have chastised me, but he acknowledged the quality of my work and my strong determination to succeed. I was a dedicated student. In fact, I studied around the clock and typically slept only about 4 hours a night.

Some nights, I would pull an all-nighter, working on my homework, then shower and get ready for work the next day, leaving the house at 6:15 am to arrive at work by 7:00 am.

My thoughts often wandered back to my childhood days when I would watch my father rise early every morning and head to work at 6:00 am. This early-rising habit was ingrained in my sister and me, and we too became early risers.

I was determined to succeed and not become a statistic. I kept my vision of becoming a professional businesswoman at the forefront of my mind at all times. No matter what obstacles arose, I was committed to making it happen. In life, you can either find excuses or find a way—I chose to find a way.

When term papers were due, I would even take my homework to work and do it on my breaks and lunch hours instead of going out with my friends. Several co-workers, who did not see the vision that I saw, would jokingly make comments such as "Why are you taking all of those college classes? You are not going to get promoted - you will still be in the same department with the rest of us!" My dear friend Sandy seemed to understand what I was trying to accomplish, and she was a great encourager to me. It was so refreshing to have a friend like Sandy who truly understood me.

Earl, the co-worker who inspired me in the first place, was also diligently moving forward to graduate in May of 1976 as well. It was a very tough road, but praise to God, we made it!

Here are photos that were taken on May 19, 1976 of us at the Washington University commencement ceremony. Daughter Nina is holding my hand below. She was 5 years old when I graduated from college.

CHAPTER 13

THE WRONG HUSBAND

Another crucial lesson I learned along my life's journey is the importance of pre-marital counseling, prayer, and seeking the Lord's blessings over the decision to marry.

After moving to University City, Missouri, we lived within walking distance of our oldest sister Verla and her husband Kenneth Johnston, and their family. The Johnstons had recently purchased a charming and spacious two-story Tudor-style home with a large backyard, perfect for the children to play with their Great Dane named Pax.

Visiting them was always a joyous occasion. All my nieces and nephews loved holding baby Nina, creating a sense of déjà vu as just a few years prior, I had cradled each of them in my arms. Valastein, the eldest niece, was only a few years younger than Beverly and me.

I fondly recall her high school days when she used to ride with me in my cool blue Mustang. One day, while we were laughing and chatting, enjoying ourselves so much that I misjudged the distance from an approaching garbage truck. Smash! Oh no! My Mustang had a big dent! Thankfully, no one was hurt. After the accident, Val and I couldn't stop laughing as we recounted the incident over and over.

Within weeks of filing a claim with my insurance company, the Mustang was repaired and back on the road. The next time I picked up Val, it was to attend choir rehearsal together. Since moving to University City, we all attended a newly established local church just ten minutes away.

We loved the sermons, choir, and the vibrant congregation. Dr. Curtis Duncan, who was the music teacher at University City High School, also served as the musical director of our church. Dr. Duncan, who earned a PhD from the University of Chicago, was exceptionally gifted in music.

We were fortunate to sing under his direction. He and his wife Doris were not only exemplary parents to their own children but also devoted countless hours to mentoring young people, teaching them musical techniques in voice and instrumental performance.

There was a young man from Ohio who started attending our church. He had an identical twin brother. One day, Dr. Duncan asked for volunteers to audition for a challenging solo. Suddenly, a remarkably elegant male voice sang the song with strength and controlled volume, as if he were a star at the Muny Opera! He held the notes for what seemed like an eternity before taking his next breath. Without further ado, he completely nailed the musical solo!

After choir rehearsal, we all gathered around to congratulate him on his outstanding singing talent. My niece Val suggested, "Marian, why don't you give him your phone number since he asked for it? He seems like a nice Christian man, and he's kind of cute too!" I decided to wait a couple of weeks to see if he was serious before giving him my number. After the third choir rehearsal, I gave him my phone number with permission to call me.

He was surprised to learn how busy and productive my schedule was. He joked, "When do you ever have fun? All you do is work and go to school!" He had a great sense of humor, a charming demeanor, and above all, he appeared to be a man of faith who professed his salvation through Jesus Christ. Alongside his beautiful singing voice, this was one of his most outstanding traits.

He always treated my daughter with respect and kindness, as if she were his own. This impressed me greatly, as I had promised Nina when she was just a baby that I would marry and give her a father. Within about six months, we walked down the aisle of my home church as husband and wife.

During the weeks of planning the wedding, I was filled with happiness. However, Mother Lovie had reservations about the marriage. At the reception, I began to question my decision when I discovered that this man had a drinking problem. He was so intoxicated that he barely noticed my presence.

The next morning, he woke up and was unexpectedly kind. However, I realized he wasn't the type of man I wanted to be married to, and suddenly I felt trapped. I should have heeded Mother Lovie's deep intuition. Why hadn't I sought premarital counseling? Most importantly, why hadn't I sought confirmation from the Lord regarding His plan for my life?

I purposely choose not to mention his name, as emotional scars from this experience have long been buried in my memory. I share these details now in hopes of enlightening other women who may face similar situations.

This "wrong husband" suffered from a complex of having a big ego and low self-esteem. He became threatened by my goal-oriented nature and determination to succeed in my career. I remember one evening when he arrived late to pick me up from Washington University.

I was the last person standing outside with an armful of heavy textbooks when he finally arrived. I asked him why he was so late, and he became enraged. Suddenly, he accelerated the car on Highway 40 westbound toward McKnight Rd. He reached over and grabbed my neck in his elbow, saying, "I'm going to kill myself and take you with me!"

At that moment, I realized this man was unstable, and I knew I had to find a way out of this situation. I prayed earnestly to the Lord for deliverance, promising never to make such a mistake again.

It wasn't long before I filed for divorce and obtained a restraining order, marking a terrible chapter characterized by the forbidden three "A" words: Abuse, Addiction, and Alcoholism. I vividly recall sitting across from my attorney, declaring, "I never want to get married again!" The attorney was astonished as I shared details of the experience.

The year before graduating from Washington University at 24, I had saved enough for a down payment on my first home—a charming brick bungalow in Rock Hill, MO. Finally, my daughter Nina had a place to call her own. Decorating her room with "Holly Hobbie" decor brought us immense joy.

Her room was adorned with white French provincial furniture, a tea table with little teacups and saucers, and cherished dolls like Raggedy Ann, Andy, Baby Alive, alongside other stuffed animals. Nina loved her little pretend kitchen tucked in the corner. She was genuinely happy there.

Nina's best friend, Robin, lived directly across the street in our friendly, family-oriented neighborhood. Each weekday, after picking up Nina from preschool after work, we'd return home, grateful to the Lord for His provisions.

Meanwhile, my sister Beverly and her husband Edward celebrated four years of marital bliss. Beverly juggled earning a Business degree from St. Louis University with managing a dental office, while Edward pursued his Photography degree from Webster University and worked at the County courthouse in Clayton, MO. I was glad to see Beverly happily married. As for me, I was content being the best mother I could be to Nina and focused on my career goal of excelling in corporate America. The thought of remarriage couldn't have been further from my mind.

CHAPTER 14

HOUSES OF HIGHER LEARNING

When I earned my degree from Washington University, I initially aimed to pursue a Master's and PhD in Psychology, driven by my dream of becoming an Industrial Psychologist. However, my experience at the Bell System revealed my true compatibility with Business Management and Marketing.

Fortunately, my application for the Bell System's tuition reimbursement program was approved, enabling me to attend Webster University for a Master's Degree in Business. Time became crucial, and I felt an internal pressure to intensify my efforts. Thus, I embarked on a rigorous schedule, taking 15-16 unit courses each semester while balancing full-time work at AT&T and caring for my young daughter, Nina, now in 1st grade.

I found business studies fascinating and engaging. I excelled swiftly through the program, earning my Master's Degree exactly 2 years and 2 months after graduating from Washington University. Celebrating my 27th birthday shortly after, I was delighted by a surprise party hosted by friends Sandy and Jerome Givens to commemorate both events. During this time, several professors praised my dedication, noting that I maintained a strong academic record with the lowest grade being a "B". They encouraged me to pursue corporate opportunities for which I was qualified.

While grateful for their feedback, my primary drive stemmed from the promise I made to Nina when she was a baby. I was determined to succeed, steadfast in my resolve never to quit or become a statistic of single parenthood dependent on government support. I believed God had endowed me with intelligence, skills, and a strong work ethic, which I honored by placing my faith in His promises. Though the journey was arduous, with many sleepless nights and overwhelming moments, I pressed onward. Finally, there was light at the end of the tunnel.

Through this experience, I learned something that has stuck with me over the years:

If You Don't Stand Up For Yourself in this World—No One Else is Going to Stand Up For You!

CHAPTER 15

PROFESSIONAL BUSINESS MOM

Armed with two diplomas and transcripts earned over that two and a half year period, I walked into Ralph Gordon's office, the Department Manager of my newly assigned division. Unfortunately, it was a lateral move, not a promotion.

Summoning all my courage, I greeted Ralph nervously, and he extended a handshake, inviting me to take a seat. "What brings you to my office today, Marian?" he asked.

"Firstly, Ralph, I'd like to share with you my recent accomplishments," I began, handing him my diplomas. Ralph's eyebrows lifted as he examined the first diploma from Washington University, indicating my graduation on May 19, 1976, followed by the Master's Degree in Business from Webster University on July 28, 1978. He also glanced at my grades on the accompanying transcripts.

"Marian, this is quite impressive!" Ralph exclaimed. "Your dedication and drive are evident." He then inquired about my aspirations.

"Ralph, I appreciate my role here and the opportunities it has provided over the past five years," I replied. "But this is just a stepping stone for me. With my work ethic and the sacrifices I've made—spending the past six years attending night school—I aim to launch a management career within this corporation. I'm seeking your recommendation to join the Bell System Management Training Program."

"Unfortunately, there's a hiring freeze on that program," Ralph lamented.

A few weeks later, I realized that if I didn't advocate for myself, no one else would. That's when I moved to phase two of my plan: writing a compelling letter on an IBM Electric Typewriter. Addressed to Mr. Nielson, Director of Operations for the Southwestern Region, with a cc to Lee Davis - this was a bold move.

These men were at the pinnacle of the company, overseeing thousands of employees across five states. Mr. Nielson's office was typically off-limits to employees like me; I had bypassed Ralph Gordon, my department manager, responsible for 8-10 supervisors and over 400 employees, including my direct supervisor.

Throughout this period, I prayed earnestly to the Lord, asking Him to guide my words and secure a meeting where I could share my story and be considered for the Management Trainee Program. I reasoned, what did I have to lose? Recalling the verse, "No weapon formed against me shall prosper," I gathered courage despite feeling nervous about stepping far outside my comfort zone. After reviewing and restructuring specific paragraphs, I signed my name and sent the letter through inter-company mail.

Two days later, my heart raced with anticipation. Had they received and read my letter? I wondered about their reaction and how they would respond.

Soon after, Lee Davis—a tall, energetic man—swiftly entered our department and exchanged words with Ralph Gordon.

Bracing myself for what might follow, I prayed silently. The worst-case scenario flashed in my mind: termination for insubordination. An hour later, my desk phone rang. It was Ralph Gordon's secretary, summoning me to his office.

"Marian, how could you have the audacity to write a letter to Mr. Nielsen and Mr. Davis? This is beyond your authority," Ralph exclaimed. "Lee Davis is furious, and now I'm left to deal with the fallout of your actions. He wants to meet with you personally in his office at 2:00 pm this afternoon."

My heart raced, palms sweating as I struggled to process my emotions. Fighting back tears, I tried to maintain composure. "Oh Lord, what have I gotten myself into?" I silently questioned, rising from my chair and making the long walk back to my office desk. The office seemed filled with whispers and murmurs from coworkers who had witnessed my reprimand from Ralph Gordon and now anticipated my meeting with Lee Davis.

"Dear God, please guide me as I enter this meeting with Lee Davis." From a Biblical perspective, I felt somewhat like David facing Goliath. Lee Davis, a dynamic leader, motioned for me to take a seat in one of the chairs before his desk.

On a scale of 1 to 10, his frustration seemed to be at an 8, understandably burdened by significant corporate responsibilities. He didn't have time for what he saw as a disruption caused by a small, determined woman who had sent a letter to the head of the Southwestern Region. "This was highly inappropriate," Lee Davis stated firmly. As he spoke in an irritated tone, I recalled the promise I made to my baby in the bassinet: to complete my education, earning a BS and MBA, for a prosperous career to provide for her. I reminded myself that God is my provider and will never abandon me (Philippians 4:19).

I closed my eyes briefly, took a deep breath, and envisioned myself as part of the Management Trainee Program.

Suddenly, Lee Davis shifted his focus to the copy of the letter I had sent. "Look at this. I can't believe you sent this to the company's top leadership. There are even punctuation errors. How do you justify this serious breach?"

"Mr. Davis, I acknowledge that I exceeded my authority by sending this letter up the corporate chain, including to you."

"A few weeks ago," I continued, "I met with Ralph Gordon to request consideration for the management trainee program, only to be informed of a hiring freeze. This was deeply disappointing after dedicating six years to surpassing the qualifications for this opportunity."

Suddenly, Lee Davis reached into the manila file folder on his desk and pulled out my company performance reviews. "I've reviewed all your employee evaluations from your supervisors since you started here. It's clear you've always been an exemplary employee in terms of job performance," he began.

"Ralph Gordon speaks highly of you as an asset to his team. It seems you're someone who quietly gets the job done with pride in both yourself and your work here at AT&T. Until now, I had no idea you were carrying such a heavy load outside your eight-hour workday."

He asked how I managed to achieve so much educationally over the past few years while maintaining excellent attendance and delivering quality work daily. I explained my faith in God and unwavering goal of succeeding in business, even if it meant considering opportunities outside AT&T, where I preferred to stay. Lee Davis stressed the importance of maintaining a balanced lifestyle to avoid "corporate burnout," sharing stories of his travels and hobbies with his wife. I mentioned the joys and challenges of being a single mom, which surprised him, and all the promises I made to my daughter about becoming a successful businesswoman and mother. At the end of our meeting, Lee Davis didn't make promises but requested a current resume by week's end.

Fulfilling the promise I made to my daughter Nina

When you confront someone, first focus on how God would want you to treat them. Next, find a quality in that person to admire. Once you do these two steps, you won't have time to think about yourself or worry about what "they" are thinking of you.

About a month later, I was called into Ralph Gordon's office again. "What have I done now?" I joked. "Please take a seat, Marian," Ralph said with a twinkle in his eye, motioning toward a chair.

He opened an envelope addressed to him on his desk and began reading a request for an interview with H. Lee Cassidy, Division Manager of the Account Management Team. I was thrilled! "Just one thing, Ralph," I asked, "what exactly does the account management group do?"

"The Account Management Team oversees the Marketing, Sales, and Public Relations functions of our company," Ralph explained. "They establish and maintain relationships with our major business clients across Missouri, Oklahoma, Kansas, Arkansas, and Texas. It's a critical organization for maintaining our key corporate client alliances."

"Lee Cassidy has reviewed your resume and wants to meet with you to discuss a recent opening in his division," Ralph continued. "Should I inform Mr. Cassidy that you're interested in interviewing for the position?"

"Yes, absolutely!" I replied eagerly.

Soon after, some colleagues introduced me to a concept I hadn't encountered before: the "Good Ole Boys club." They described it as a tight-knit group of W.A.S.P. (White Anglo-Saxon Protestant) men, supported administratively by outgoing women who handled their correspondence, travel arrangements, expense reports, and other tasks. I received cautionary advice from others who warned me to be careful.

They believed the company had set me up for failure, predicting challenges as both the first black person and woman in this division. They cautioned that the existing secretaries might resent my credentials and authority, potentially making it difficult for them to support me.

"Watch your back, Marian," they emphasized.

As I entered a very plush division of the company, I thought, "So, this is how the other people live!" Until that moment, I never realized such luxury existed there. Stepping through the double doors, I felt exhilarated yet somewhat apprehensive, holding my shoulders back as I glided through the suite. I was warmly greeted by Sandy, an enthusiastic young woman with red hair, freckles, and a broad Texas smile. Since I had arrived 20 minutes early, she invited me to take a seat and informed me that Mr. Cassidy would be with me shortly.

As I sat there, my mind raced with gratitude to the Lord for bringing me so far from where I started. It was a monumental journey from praying at 16 to get hired at the five-and-dime store, to wandering the fields near the Edgewood Children's Center. From those days to this moment, where I was about to interview for a position I had worked hard to qualify for, I silently thanked God for all the blessings that had brought me here.

"Nice to meet you, Marian," said Mr. Cassidy after his secretary, Sandy Powell, formally introduced us. "Please, have a seat." Mr. Cassidy exuded leadership not only in his demeanor and attitude but also in his professional appearance, towering over the other executives with his stature exceeding six feet four inches tall.

His attire was professional yet approachable, with various certificates, awards, and family photos tastefully displayed throughout his expansive office. During the interview, Mr. Cassidy aimed to establish rapport and understand the mindset and attitude I would bring to his organization. He expressed admiration for my work ethic and credentials, complimenting the achievements detailed in my resume and company records. Mr. Cassidy inquired about my career goals and willingness to travel, including trips to AT&T's Corporate Training Center in New Hope, New Jersey, and across the five states of the Southwestern Region. Despite having flown only once before, on a vacation in 1974, I eagerly looked forward to business travel.

I felt confident and relaxed throughout the interview, believing the open position aligned well with my skills and personality. Exiting the interview, I was so elated that I practically jumped for joy in the elevator!

About three days later, I was offered the job, and preparations for my promotion began. Ralph Gordon congratulated me, emphasizing the significant increase in income—more than triple my current salary. After years in a clerical role at AT&T, I felt blessed to have pursued advanced education, qualifying me to compete for a professional position in a prestigious organization. Having my own office among top-level employees recruited from Ivy League schools and major corporations felt like a true testament to God's blessings. "With God, all things are possible" (Philippians 4:13).

Reviews Are Gold to Authors:

Would you consider leaving a review on Amazon?

CHAPTER 16
THE FIRST RIGHT HUSBAND

It was an exceptionally cold day, and the commute on Highway 40 from Rock Hill, MO to Ballwin, MO was treacherous. Fortunately, I had recently equipped my brand new Chevrolet Caprice Classic with radial snow tires, anticipating such conditions. With temperatures well below zero and biting winds, we hurriedly sought refuge in the massive building at 1111 Woodsmill Rd. Surely, the company cafeteria would see record sales today—none of us wanted to deal with ice-covered windshields during lunch or after work!

Concerned about the severe weather, I requested a brief meeting with Lee Cassidy in his office to explain why I was hesitant to undertake another business trip to New Hope, New Jersey. "The snow is heavy and visibility is poor," I explained, "and as a single mom, my daughter depends on me." Lee reassured me, "When you fly, you rise above the weather."

Thankfully, my sister Beverly and friend Pat were able to care for my daughter while I traveled for more business training in New Jersey. Little did I know, New Hope would bring new opportunities into my life that week.

Arriving at the AT&T Corporate Training Center, I felt a sense of liberation in the air. On the chartered bus from the airport, I struck up a conversation with Ruth, a kind lady from Texas who, like me, worked at AT&T and juggled family responsibilities. We quickly bonded and agreed to team up for meals each day.

As I walked through the expansive lobby toward the main building, a friendly man with a warm smile passed by carrying his luggage. We exchanged courteous greetings, and I noticed his name tag: Frank Graham. "What a coincidence," I thought silently. I recalled a Frank Graham from my childhood in Webster Groves, Missouri.

The next day, after dinner, Ruth and I ventured onto the tennis court to burn off a few calories. Although I was a novice, Ruth graciously adjusted her game to accommodate me. Meanwhile, Frank Graham was on another court, playing exceptionally well.

I resolved to approach him the following day and inquire if he had grown up in Webster Groves, Missouri. I wanted to be cautious not to sound foolish or embarrass myself—though the thought of it made me laugh out loud!

The next morning, as I walked down the hallway toward breakfast, Frank Graham was heading in the same direction. "Good morning! How are you?" he greeted.

"Fine!" I replied. "By the way, Frank, are you by any chance the Frank Graham who grew up in Webster Groves, Missouri?" At the same time, he asked, "Don't you have a little sister named Beverly, and aren't you one of the West girls?"

To my relief, I sighed, "Yes, I am formerly Marian West, and I do have a sister named Beverly, though she's not so little anymore!" We both laughed heartily.

We sat down together for breakfast, joined of course by Ruth. Frank and I shared with Ruth how his father, Mr. McKinley Graham, had served as a deacon at the same church where my father was the Associate Pastor. Additionally, Frank's mother, Mrs. Aleina Graham, sang in the Old Community Baptist Church Choir alongside my late mother, Mrs. Rose West. Ruth was fascinated by our connection!

With Frank being six years my senior, I had always thought of him as Ronnie and Gregory Graham's older brother when I was a child. For instance, while I was in 6th grade, he was preparing for college. Fast forward to all these years later, it felt like we were on equal footing, and our age difference didn't seem to matter.

As I mentioned earlier, New Hope, New Jersey brought new hope not just for me, but also for Frank Graham. We discussed how it was no coincidence that we both ended up at the BSTC Bel System Training Center at the same time.

Frank Graham and me with a business associate

Originally scheduled to attend later in the spring, Frank's director at AT&T made a last-minute decision when another employee scheduled to go had an emergency, sending Frank instead. In contrast, despite my efforts to dissuade Lee Cassidy from sending me to New Jersey in harsh winter weather, I found myself there nonetheless.

Each day during our mealtime meetings, more "coincidences" unfolded. "So, what have you been doing all these years, Frank? It's hard to believe it's been more than 15 years since I last saw you!"

"So much has happened," Frank replied. "I served 6 years in the United States Air Force, traveled all over the world, went to college, got married, became a father. Unfortunately, the marriage ended in a tumultuous divorce. Most recently, AT&T promoted me and transferred me back to the St. Louis area. I just closed escrow on a home in Rock Hill, MO, and I have a little son named Alex."

"You do?" I exclaimed. "I also bought a home in Rock Hill, MO, divorced three years ago, and have a little girl named Nina!"

Little did I know, this was the beginning of one of the most beautiful relationships I could have ever imagined up to that point in my life. In later years, I practically melted when I overheard a conversation Frank was having with our children about our first meeting in January 1978 at the Bell System Training Center in New Hope, New Jersey.

"When I met your mom, it was love at first sight," Frank said to Alex and Nina. He described me as a beautiful, elegant, and statuesque young woman! He was so confident in himself that my height (5'11") didn't bother him at all, even though he stood approximately 5'10".

I had always dated men who were at least 6'2", but I overlooked the height difference because Frank was the man of my dreams—a person with qualities I never thought I'd find in one man. To me, he was a giant among men. Together, we learned that love knows no height. As Frank would say, "Height isn't what's important; it's a person's attitude that counts the most."

Upon returning to Missouri, I hoped that our fairy tale wouldn't come to an end. And it didn't. Frank and I were highly compatible, and shared so much in common. Even our children blended well together. We cherished each other's company and envisioned spending the rest of our lives together.

After nurturing a loving and caring relationship for nearly a year, we united our lives in marriage. It was a private ceremony, on a cold winter's day, in a small church in Iowa. Because it was a second marriage for both of us, we decided to forego any grand ceremonies with bridesmaids, groomsmen, and all the elaborate details.

Our intimate wedding was without a professional photographer, a large pictorial album, or a vast guest list. The only attendees were the pastor, the organist, Alex, Nina, Frank's sister Bonnie, her husband Jim, Frank, and Marian! We also legally adopted each other's children, making me the legal mother of his son Alex, and Frank the legal father of Nina.

For our honeymoon, we chose the Bahamas! It was the most romantic, breathtaking, and rejuvenating vacations of my life! Frank and I had an incredible time together in the Bahamas. The love and affection we shared were absolutely off the charts! It was the kind of love we both deserved.

Frank and I were cut from the same cloth—we were both generous and kind-hearted, giving without expecting anything in return. He delighted in showing me new sights and scenery I had never seen before. We loved spending time on the beach, searching for seashells, dining at restaurants, and exploring the Grand Bahama Islands. Our deep love for each other was matched by our mutual respect and admiration.

At last, we had a complete and beautiful family. All four of us were very happy! Of course, we had certain housekeeping details to wrap up. The little brick bungalow that I bought as a home for Nina and me was put up for sale. Fortunately, my dear younger sister Beverly and her husband Edward were able to purchase it as first-time homeowners.

Some of the furnishings were taken with us, and the rest we sold to relatives and friends. We fit very well into Frank's ranch-style, brick home with a custom swimming pool in the backyard. It was ideal for a family of four: Father, Mother, Sister, and Brother. What a great family we were! We thanked God for His blessings.

One day, Frank was in the pool with Alex and Nina, having a great time swimming and splashing water all over the deck! As for me, a non-swimmer, I sat on the chaise lounge relaxing. Later on, everyone took a break, and I decided that I was going to surprise Frank and the children by getting in the pool.

Suddenly, I panicked and was overcome by the water. "Daddy, Daddy, come quickly! Mommy is in the pool, and she can't swim. Help her!" screamed Nina and Alex. Without thinking, Frank jumped into the pool to rescue me, and we both went down. Finally, he convinced me to stop struggling, and he brought me up to safety. Once the rescue was over, Frank and I both cried tears of relief and joy that the outcome had been positive and not the opposite.

Frank told me later that if he had not acted so suddenly and taken a moment to think first, he could have handed me a pole to grab onto, and it would have been easier to pull me out of the pool. However, I shuddered to think how dumb it was for me to think I was surprising them when it could have been a surprise tragedy instead. Another thing I should have done was to have at least put on a life vest. In reality, I was very grateful that Frank Graham saved my life that day, risking his own life so that I might live.

Life was good—really good! For family vacations, we visited places on the West Coast, such as California and Arizona. In the fall, we went back east to see the beautiful changing leaves of the Pocono Mountains in Pennsylvania, and sometimes to New York. We enjoyed hosting fabulous holiday dinners and children's birthday parties, which were always spectacular.

Frank enjoyed entertaining his father, brothers, and extended family. His first cousin Eddie, and his family would often come over to our barbecues and poolside gatherings and reminisce about the days when Eddie used to create beautiful winter wonderland ice sculptures on the front lawn, which fascinated all of us in the neighborhood. By then, Eddie was a successful architect and, a few years prior, had become one of the first black students to graduate from Washington University School of Architecture.

Eddie's older brother, George, married a distant cousin of mine named Alice Frazier. They had a daughter named Gail and sons Peter and Nick. Eddie and George's two sisters, Margaret and Vertie, were two of the sweetest ladies who had known Beverly and me since we were born. We always felt very close to and admired them. Vertie married Lloyd Burgett and had one son named Lloyd after his father. Margaret married and had a daughter named Priscilla, whom we all played with while living on Elm Ave.

George was a very distinguished speaker and eventually became the associate pastor of Old Community Baptist Church after my father died. This was another thing Frank and I had in common—we grew up in the same town. We knew many of the same people and were even related to some of the same people on opposite sides of the family.

Frank was such a great family man—the type of man I always dreamed of marrying someday. Frank Graham was the right husband for me. He and I were so close that many times we would even finish each other's sentences. He was a man of great strength under control, like the Rock of Gibraltar.

One time, we were on our way home from a dinner date, and Frank said something to me that I will never forget as long as I live. We were discussing how strong and independent we both were when Frank said,

"Marian, you know how much I love you, and there is nothing that I would not do for you. However, because both of us are strong and independent, one of us has to give, and it is not going to be me!"

This statement made me laugh so hard, especially the way he said it! However, Frank was so right—a marriage can't have two heads. From that moment on, I gladly and willingly submitted to my wonderful husband.

I responded, "Frank, you can be the head, but I am going to be the neck that turns the head!"

It was such a relief for me to be married to a man who was a leader that I was willing to follow. It felt as though a huge weight had been lifted off my shoulders to have a man I could rely on, learn from, and grow with. What a tremendous blessing that I certainly did not take lightly.

Frank was a highly intelligent and diligent student. One day, while going through some boxes in the garage, I came across some old report cards and school records that belonged to my husband, Frank Graham, and I was amazed at what I read.

- Calculus 1 - A
- Calculus 2 - A
- Analytical Geometry - A

Wow! Frank must be a left-brainer, I thought. Then I read further and saw the following:

- English - A
- Literature - A
- History - A

His penmanship was outstanding as well. Back in the days when he was a paperboy selling the San Francisco Chronicle, Frank was impressed with the beautiful calligraphy that was used in the paper. In his spare time, he would diligently practice until he was able to write exactly like that, freehand - without the use of a stencil or any aid!

During holidays and birthdays, it was always a special treat for our family and friends to receive a handwritten card that displayed a beautifully written version of their names personally handcrafted by Frank. It was even more exquisite than the card itself!

Even though he exhibited a quiet, unpretentious demeanor, Frank Graham was a brilliant man and an extremely well-balanced thinker, as well as a man of humility. He did not call attention to his own accomplishments. He did not believe in self-exaltation or thinking he was higher than another person. Frank had been gifted by God in so many ways, and he never forgot where he came from.

Frank grew up in the 50s and 60s, prior to the desegregation of the school system. His graduating class was the first to integrate the schools after the law ended segregation. Circumstances led Frank's mother to move to California with her three sons, Frank, Gregory, and Ronnie. In California, they lived with their older sister Bernadine and her husband, Tom Glover.

While living in California, a teacher discovered that Frank Graham had scored the highest on the SAT. Shortly afterward, he was one of the few students selected to attend an exclusive organization called All American Boys State. Frank was the only black student who was chosen.

He excelled greatly there and thrived in the new environment. If his dear sweet mother had not died suddenly, causing Frank tremendous grief and loss of focus, he would not have declined the four-year full-ride scholarship offered to him by Stanford University.

Devastated by the loss of their mother, their key inspiration, Frank and his brothers flew with their older sister Bernadine back to Missouri to live with their beloved father, McKinley Graham, in their modest red brick home on Almentor Place in Webster Groves, MO. As the oldest son, Frank was very diligent in looking out for the care and protection of his two younger brothers. This experience probably prepared him for fatherhood in the future.

CHAPTER 17

CULTURE SHOCK

As the years went by, Frank and I continued to enjoy our careers at AT&T. He drove to his office every day in Clayton, Missouri, while I commuted to my office in Ballwin, MO. Whenever either of us had to travel out of town on company business trips, we coordinated our schedules to ensure that at least one parent would be home with Alex and Nina. It was important to us that our children never felt abandoned and had the continuity of at least one parent at home.

Alex especially needed to know he was loved and cared for, as he had experienced abandonment in his early years when his biological mother left him in harm's way. This led to Alex being placed in several foster homes, which devastated Frank. He hired the best attorney and gained custody of his highly intelligent and impressionable son, who exhibited a warm smile despite the difficult circumstances he had encountered. "There is no telling what my son has had to endure in his young life," Frank would comment.

With my natural maternal instinct of protectiveness toward children and an undergraduate degree in Psychology, I recognized that Alex was suffering from serious psychological wounds that affected his self-esteem and ability to enjoy his young life and trust others completely.

I will never forget the first day Frank introduced me to 5-year-old Alex Graham. He was playing with his toys in the living room, and when he saw me, he had a huge grin on his face and began to play hide-and-seek under a blue blanket on the floor. He was the cutest little boy I had ever seen! "It is nice to meet you, Miss Marian," said little Alex as he extended his tiny hand to greet me after his father introduced us.

Alex had been staying with Frank's oldest sister Bonnie and her husband Jim while Frank worked and traveled for AT&T. It was quite evident that Bonnie and Jim had instilled a lot of love, time, and energy into teaching their little nephew. They were in their retirement years and welcomed the option of having a lively child around their household. Alex was a well-mannered boy, who spoke with eloquence and a high level of vocabulary, far exceeding his age. It was no surprise to me when the psychologist revealed years later that Alex's IQ was at the genius level.

Alex and I shared the birthday month of July, with our birthdays only three days apart. Despite the close range, I made it a point to have a separate celebration just for him, ensuring he felt like the center of attention and didn't have to share the limelight.

Alex and Nina became very close and had no problem with the blended-family scenario, easily accepting one another as siblings. To anyone who didn't know, we appeared to be a complete family with a father, mother, son, and daughter. Our desire was to be the best parents we could be for our two children by letting them know how much they were loved.

One day while working as the manager of the AT&T Product Display Center, a small voice in my mind indicated that I would not be in charge of this beautiful center much longer because we were going to move to California.

In reality, I didn't mind, nor did Frank, because we welcomed the opportunity to move to a warmer climate. A new setting would allow us to start fresh, where no one knew our history and we would be accepted as the Graham family.

Lo-and-behold, about a month later, Frank arrived home from work and announced that he had received an offer to work in Mission Viejo, California! When asked what I thought about it, I replied with an enthusiastic, "YES!" The only reservation I had about moving so far away was the thought of being apart from my "delayed twin" sister, Beverly. We cried for days, and even after we moved, our husbands agreed that airfare would have been cheaper than the huge telephone bills we ran up with our daily conversations. And just to think, we even got a discount from AT&T, yet the bill was still outrageous!

Otherwise, the timing for this transition was perfect for several reasons. First, the Bell System was going through a huge divestiture and breakup due to a class action lawsuit. As a result of antitrust laws, the company was forced to split up. This divestiture meant a complete restructuring of all departments and job descriptions, and many of our positions were subject to elimination.

When I went for my annual gynecological exam, I discovered that we were expecting another child in November, due on my sister Beverly's birthday! Frank, the children, and I were absolutely thrilled with the news of a new baby in the household. Alex had only one stipulation: the baby had to be a boy because he wanted a brother to play with. Of course, Nina had been asking for a little sister for years. Only time would tell who would get their wish, unless I gave birth to twins and had one of each!

The huge moving van pulled up to our home, and all the packed boxes, furniture, and household belongings were loaded onto it. Even our cars were loaded onto the van! We had a huge farewell party and then boarded the jet plane to LAX in sunny Southern California as a family. Once we arrived, I was in tears as we drove at a snail's pace from Los Angeles to Mission Viejo, California. Never in my life had I seen so much traffic. It was quite intimidating for me. Frank was driving, of course, while I navigated with a map in hand.

"Frank, doesn't Mission Viejo mean 'The Old Mission' in Spanish?"

"Yes, it does," Frank replied.

"I wonder how the town is going to look. Do you think it will be an old town?"

Frank laughed and said, "Based on what I observed during my trip out for the company interview, Mission Viejo is one of the finest places to live. In fact, they even have their own lake! The homes there are beautiful, mostly Spanish architecture with stucco and either red tile roofs or wooden shake roofs. The only thing I noticed was we would no longer have the large lots that we were accustomed to. The houses were so close together that you could reach out of your window and shake hands with your neighbors!"

The second thing I noticed was that in Mission Viejo, real estate prices were approximately two and a half times more than real estate in Missouri! With the corporate relocation program, we had the option to stay at a hotel for several weeks, giving us time to find a suitable home for our growing family at a price we could afford.

Living in Mission Viejo, the gem of Orange County, California, was a true culture shock for us. Many weeks passed before we encountered anyone who resembled us. This was before the days of Oprah, so we didn't even see other black people on television!

Coming from Webster Groves, MO, where we were used to being a minority comprising only 4% of the population, we discovered that in our new community, the minority population was less than 1%. We began to see more diversity in nearby Santa Ana and also encountered people from all over the country and the world when we visited Disneyland, which was somewhat comforting.

Our children, Alex and Nina, adjusted as best they could, although many white students at Mission Viejo schools initially rejected them based on assumptions about their race. Additionally, Mission Viejo High School emphasized prestige and fashion correctness. Many students drove BMWs their parents bought for them, and not wearing Jordache jeans, as Nina informed me, was considered a fashion faux pas. To help her feel accepted and avoid teasing about her regular nice clothes, I rushed to the Mission Viejo Mall and bought a full wardrobe of Jordache and other name-brand clothing.

One day, Frank attended a business meeting in Orange County, CA, where he met a successful businessman named Frank Morales. Frank and his wife Barbara invited us to attend a new startup church called Saddleback Community Church, which was holding worship services at a school in Laguna Hills, CA. This church was started in the home of a youthful, tall, and very slender young man named Rick Warren and his wife, Kay Warren. Little did we realize that we were becoming part of a church that would grow to be one of the largest and most influential in the world, with its pastor eventually writing one of the highest-selling books called *The Purpose Driven Life*.

Frank and I loved attending Saddleback Community Church because our entire family felt the love of God and welcomed as soon as we entered the doors. We especially enjoyed the music led by Rick Muchow, the dedicated choir director who shared his musical talents in the ministry. After every sermon, Frank would comment on the way home, saying, "I really like the way Rick teaches the word of God."

Alex also loved the church and enjoyed spending time with other boys in the youth ministry. Nina found great joy in the creative aspects of the ministry, feeling uplifted each time we attended. The diversity of the congregation was another positive aspect that we appreciated. I'm thankful that through this fellowship, Frank and I rededicated our lives to Christ, and our children accepted the Lord Jesus Christ as their Savior.

Little did we know at the time that someday Rick Warren would be called by God to comfort our family during a tragedy we never could have imagined. As you will read in the upcoming chapter, we are extremely grateful to Pastor Rick Warren for personally coming to assist us in the midst of his busy schedule. None of us will ever forget his kindness for as long as we live.

The Lord truly blessed our family with the ability to purchase two homes, and prosper greatly in Southern California. For a while, we used one of the homes as income property, which provided us with a better income tax scenario and served as a good investment for the financial future of our growing family.

Dr. Mike Akrawi and his wife, Hermine Akrawi, were two of the nicest doctors I had ever met! Each prenatal exam with them was a joyful experience. I cherished listening to the baby's heartbeat and seeing the ultrasound images of our expected newborn. Attending the weekly Lamaze classes at Mission Community Hospital allowed us to meet many couples and helped us feel connected to the community.

I thank the Lord for modern medicine, which saved me from miscarrying our precious child. One day, Frank had to rush me to the emergency room. Tests revealed that the baby was distressed and premature labor was imminent. "Oh no, it's too early. I'm only five months pregnant!" I exclaimed in pain. "Please, doctor, do everything you can to save her—please! Dr. Akrawi, please save my baby!" I cried. Thanks to a new drug called Terbutaline, the premature labor was halted. Praise the Lord for His wonderful blessings!

Three months later, Frank traveled to Los Angeles for a corporate meeting. During the lunch break, as he usually did, Frank called me. When he asked how I was doing, I mentioned experiencing Braxton Hicks contractions.

"How do you know they're not the real thing? How many minutes apart are the pains?" asked Frank.

"I'll start timing them later and let you know," I replied.

The next day, Frank and I were getting ready for our Lamaze class when suddenly I felt the strongest labor pains since giving birth to Nina ten years before! Despite being a month earlier than expected, I knew our little daughter would soon be welcomed into the world. By the time we reached the hospital, I was already more than 6 centimeters dilated, and Frank and I went straight to the Labor and Delivery floor.

Despite the intense pain, having such a supportive husband by my side was a remarkable experience. Frank coached me through the breathing techniques we had practiced in Lamaze class, looking like a doctor himself in his green gown, mask, and gloves. It was a stark contrast from ten years prior when I gave birth to my first child alone, without the father or any close family nearby. I was deeply grateful to be loved by such a caring husband and father to our children.

Moments later, Dr. Akrawi urged me to "PUSH!" Once I did, he exclaimed, "Where did this baby get this heavy head of hair from?"

"Well, my mother and sisters have lots of hair!" Frank replied.

It was true; Mrs. Aliena Graham and especially Frank's sister Bonnie had thick waist-length hair that seemed almost Native American. I pushed again, and Francesca Maria Graham was born!

She was a beautiful baby girl, letting out a wail to ensure her lungs were in excellent working condition. We had already chosen her name: Francesca, after her father Frank, and Maria, which was my first name minus the "n". Francesca was born around the time of our Lamaze class, and afterward, all the parents and the instructor came to the Labor and Delivery floor to congratulate us and welcome baby Francesca into the world. Within a few days, other classmates gave birth to their newborns as well. Because Francesca was born prematurely, the pediatrician informed us that she would need to stay in the hospital's incubator until her bilirubin count returned to normal.

It was heart-wrenching to leave our baby girl at the hospital, but the silver lining was that it was only a short distance from our home. As a family, we visited her several times a day. Finally, about three or four days later, we dressed Francesca in a beautiful yellow one-piece suit and brought her home on a glorious, sunny Southern California day. There wasn't a cloud in the sky. On that day, we thanked the Lord for the victory He had provided for our family.

Transitioning to being a stay-at-home mom was a joy amidst the challenges of being over 2,000 miles away from home and all our roots. It was a blessing to raise our children without the distractions of a demanding career during that phase of my life. The benefits and positive outcomes for our children were priceless.

Every year, Grandpa McKinley Graham visited us for three to four weeks at a time. Margaret Works, Grandpa's niece who also moved to California, often visited during his stays. Eventually, my older sisters Verla and Mary, along with Frank's oldest sister Bernadine Glover and her husband, also moved to California. Before long, Southern California became the gathering place for our family reunions.

CHAPTER 18

GOD WHY DO YOU TAKE AWAY THE GOOD HUSBANDS?

By the time Francesca turned one-year-old, Frank and I had already purchased a brand new home in the beautiful Whelan Ranch area of Oceanside, CA. The home was spacious enough to accommodate our growing family. We made this move 45 miles south because Frank had recently been transferred to the AT&T office in downtown San Diego, CA.

Oceanside proved to be an ideal town for us. Not only did it shorten Frank's commute, but it also positioned us centrally between our friends in Orange County and our relatives in Riverside County. To celebrate Francesca's first birthday and our new home, we threw a huge party. Many of the babies and parents from our Lamaze class in Mission Viejo attended, and we still cherish the photos of all the one-year-old "Lamaze Graduates" taken that day. It's amazing to think that they are all grown now, with many married and having children of their own.

Living in Whelan Ranch was enjoyable because every home was occupied by young families with children around the same ages as ours.

The homeowners' committee, organized many fun activities for the community, including an Easter egg hunt.

By the time Francesca turned five years old, Alex and Nina were 14 and 15 years old and in high school. Through our children, Frank and I met many wonderful parents who became lifelong friends, such as Walter and Wilma Stamps, whose daughter Aris was friends with Francesca since kindergarten. This couple played an integral role in our lives, and we remain close friends to this day, almost like family.

We were fortunate to become members of another wonderful local church, and with Frank's sister and brother-in-law living around the corner from us, we felt our family had a well-balanced life. Finally, Frank and I could plan romantic getaways without worrying about how our children would be cared for during our absence. We were truly blessed.

A few months later, my beautiful first-born daughter, Nina, joined me on a shopping trip to the local grocery store. After parking the car, I took a moment to gather my thoughts before sharing some news with her.

"Mom, are you kidding me?" Nina asked in a distressed tone. "Are you really pregnant? I'm 16 years old, and now you're telling me you're having another baby?!"

Once we arrived home and I shared the news with our other two children, Alex responded by informing me that if I brought home another girl and not a baby brother next time, he was going to go on strike and not speak to us for two weeks! Of course, Francesca was thrilled to know that she was going to have a little sister or brother closer to her age than her older siblings.

It turned out that several friends in the neighborhood were also expecting babies, and we jokingly agreed that "it must have been something in the water!" Over the next few months, as our child grew within me, Frank looked at me and said, "I can't believe all of this is going to come through you and your svelte frame!" He was right, because by the 5th month, my profile looked as large as it did in the 9th month of my previous pregnancies.

The Rotary Club gave us a surprise baby shower, and later in the week, my friend Kathy Pacheco and several ladies from the church threw us another baby shower! That week was lots of fun. However, I was beginning to feel drained of energy and was looking forward to the delivery of our fourth child, due on Frank's birthday of May 7th. This little baby was eager to come into the world, as I felt the kicking and somersaults in preparation for the big arrival!

On May 2nd, I couldn't believe the amount of Shakey's pizza I consumed—it was certainly enough for three people. Twenty-four hours later, Frank and I were at Tri-City Medical Center for the very familiar scenario of bringing a wonderful baby into the world! With every labor pain, the intensity grew to the point that, as a distraction, I began to beat into Frank's back with my fists, especially when the doctor had the audacity to use forceps during the contractions!

Joyfully, on May 3rd, just minutes before midnight, we welcomed our beautiful precious daughter Brittany into the world. She let out a robust and healthy cry, as only a newborn can do!

Brittany was healthy and happy from the start, weighing in at 8 pounds and born completely full-term, making her the first child I gave birth to who didn't need an incubator. It was a blessing to see her thriving!

Hours later, as we walked back from the nursery, we were congratulated by our neighbor, Bob Warnamuende, who mentioned that his wife, Gilda, was also about to deliver. Their baby was born on Cinco de Mayo!

Our entire family gathered around Brittany, taking turns holding her carefully. She was a cheerful and quick learner, surrounded by her older siblings constantly. Now our family felt complete—Mother, Father, Son, Daughter #1, Daughter #2, and Daughter #3. We were one big happy family, often reminded by others of the family on The Cosby Show. Counting our blessings, we thanked God for His provisions. Life was good!

Frank enjoyed feeding 10-month-old Brittany in her high chair, delighted by how eagerly she gobbled up every spoonful of baby food. "I'm glad to see our baby has such a good appetite and isn't picky!" he remarked. After mealtime, Frank and Brittany played a game where she crawled fast and he chased her, both laughing heartily. Witnessing this loving interaction between father and daughter filled me with joy.

It was truly wonderful to have a husband who let his guard down and connected with his children on the floor. Frank took off from work that Friday and the following Monday so we could travel to celebrate our 7th anniversary, which was the next day, March 12th.

With great anticipation, we had planned every detail for the children's care and arranged for the housekeeper to stay overnight until our return on Monday. Frank drove me around all day to run various errands, including stopping by my favorite hair salon where I was greeted by Mrs. Lottie Yates, always cheerful. Lottie recommended to me of certain hair products for me. The grocery store was our last stop, and we filled the trunk of the car to capacity with groceries. On the ride home, Frank and I talked excitedly about the quality time we were looking forward to over the weekend. Pulling up to the garage door, we decided to leave the car in the driveway and enlisted the children and housekeeper to help with the groceries so we could prepare for our vacation on time. Suddenly, Frank made a statement that greatly alarmed me.

"Marian, I need you to take me to the hospital to see a doctor. I have a pain in my chest," said Frank calmly.

First of all, my husband was like many men for whom the last words in their vocabulary would be "doctor," let alone to say both "hospital" and "doctor" in the same sentence. As I drove Frank slowly to the hospital, everything was a blur. Thankfully, the distance was short, and upon arrival, the emergency room staff placed Frank on a gurney to determine whether he was experiencing a myocardial infarction.

"Frank, when you get out of this hospital, we need to exercise more, cut back on fatty foods, and maybe you should consider leaving that stressful job so we can start our own business," I nervously rambled on.

As they began to roll Frank into the treatment room, he gently raised my left hand to his lips and affectionately kissed it. Looking up at me from the gurney, he said, "I love you, Marian," before slowly releasing my hand, almost as if in slow motion...

Within a very short period, the hospital waiting room filled with family and friends who came to support me. Tom and Bernadine Glover, my husband's sister- and brother-in-law, arrived shortly after we did. Our longtime family friends, Frank and Barbara Morales, rushed from San Juan Capistrano to Oceanside. They must have driven 90 miles an hour,

I thought. Larry and Audra Popp were also there, surrounding me with their love and assuring me that Frank would be okay. Audra, being a nurse, was in her element with the emergency room protocol. Several other family and friends were present, though I struggle to recall many names and faces due to the traumatic nature of the event.

I do remember a phone call from Frank's brother and father, anxiously seeking updates about their beloved son and brother. Unbeknownst to me, a code blue alert was sounded, and medical staff hurried to Frank's room. Suddenly, a team of four cardiologists emerged from the room. As they approached me, they removed their surgical masks, their faces solemn and sorrowful. The chief cardiologist looked directly into my eyes and became the bearer of the devastating news.

"Frank fought a valiant fight. His last words were, 'Hang in there, keep fighting for you, CAN do it.' I'm sorry, Mrs. Graham, we did everything we could to save your husband. We extend our deepest sympathy to you and your children."

At that moment, I collapsed onto the floor of the hospital waiting room, overcome with sorrow and despair. Tears streamed down my face uncontrollably, and I struggled to catch my breath, hyperventilating with grief. When asked to identify my husband's body, I cried out in anguish, "No! No! I can't do that."

Thankfully, Frank Morales came to my rescue, volunteering to perform the task. He returned with the confirmation that it was indeed the body of my beloved husband, Frank Graham, in the morgue at Tri-City Medical Center Hospital. It was a heartbreaking moment for everyone who had gathered. When our friends drove me home, the children immediately asked where their beloved daddy was.

In a state of absolute shock, I remained awake for over 72 hours without any sleep. My friend Lois Beeman called and urged me to turn on the radio. There, Pastor E.V. Hill from Los Angeles was delivering a sermon titled "Trust God."

Ironically, Pastor Hill spoke of losing his own wife and how he found solace in trusting God through his grief. "Trust God," he repeated. His words echoed in my ears. Overwhelmed, I sank to the floor, pounding it with my fists. "My Lord, why did you take the good men and leave the bums walking the streets?" I cried out in anger towards God. It was the first and only time in my life that I felt such deep anger, especially directed at God.

Tears poured down my face uncontrollably, feeling as though my soul had been torn apart. I felt utterly helpless and defenseless, like a child. Reflecting on my grief, nothing could match the pain of losing Frank Graham so suddenly and unexpectedly, not even the loss of my dear father. Later, when I looked in the closet, I discovered the anniversary gifts Frank had planned to give me that weekend. Seeing them brought on even more tears. To this day, I haven't been able to bring myself to open those gifts.

My thoughts drifted back to two incidents. About three years earlier, as we headed to our timeshare at Treetop Village in the Lake of the Ozarks, Frank confided in me about a generational heart defect in the males of his family. His sister Bonnie's son and his youngest brother Ronnie had both passed away in their early twenties. Frank then said something that shook me to my core: "I doubt if I will even live to see the age of 43," he remarked. Sadly, he died on March 11, 1988, just two months shy of his forty-third birthday on May 7th. Desperately searching for answers, my mind raced back to a conversation with a friend while driving our children around town. "If something ever happened to Frank, I don't know what I would do," I had said.

The Bible teaches, "Death and life are in the power of the tongue" (Proverbs 18:21). Lord, could it have been that Frank spoke death and not life? From that point on, I chose to speak life and declare it. From that day forward, I vowed never to shed tears over anything that could be replaced. Material possessions hold no value; no matter their cost, I would have traded them all if it could have saved Frank's life. Our children lost their father, and I lost the best husband, my closest friend, lover, confidant, and the leader I respected and happily submitted to. There is simply no comparison.

A few weeks later, I dropped a diamond ring down the kitchen sink drain and didn't even gasp when it happened.

God places certain people in your life for a specific reason. The doorbell rang, and there stood a lady insisting on visiting me, though I was locked in my room, filled with grief and despair, wanting no visitors and desiring to be left alone. She introduced herself as Mrs. Earline Thornton. Was it a coincidence that I had met her only a week before at a dinner party Frank and I attended? Could she be the one who shared her story of overcoming the sudden death of her beloved husband to a massive heart attack years ago? Surely, Lord, she must be one of the few who truly understands my pain. With all the composure I could muster, I agreed to see her, and I will never regret it.

Mrs. Thornton comforted me in my sorrow. She understood my feelings and the magnitude of my loss. I didn't need to pretend with her; she knew firsthand the grief of losing a spouse. She knew what to say and what not to say. Her husband, Robert, loved her and their son, Robert Jr., with all his heart. Sadly, he delayed going to the hospital despite chest and arm pains, and it was too late. The heart that loved her so was forever silenced.

God had sent Mrs. Thornton to me as "a very present help in the time of storm" (Psalm 46:1).

Walking down that long, dreary aisle, I struggled with each step, carrying our 10-month-old baby girl Brittany on my right hip, holding hands with our six-and-a-half-year-old Francesca, and flanked by our two young teens, Nina and Alex, accompanied by my sister Beverly. Inside, I kept saying, "Lord, this wasn't supposed to happen! Frank is with you now, Lord. The body before us is just a shell."

Eternal Hills Chapel overflowed with AT&T employees, family, friends from across the country, church members, neighbors, our children's teachers, and countless community members who came to honor Frank M. Graham that day. The Eulogy was so graciously performed by Pastor Rick Warren of Saddleback Community Church. Every Sunday, Frank appreciated each sermon that Rick Warren gave. Our family was blessed and inspired when we attended the services back in the day when Saddleback Church was just getting started at a local high school.

The unbearable grief consumed me, and I spiraled into a deep depression where I no longer cared about my own existence, except for the sake of my four children, who were my reason for living. My sister Beverly, understood my situation and contacted me daily, making frequent trips to California to offer support. My other sisters, Mary and Verla, also reached out to help.

I am forever grateful for the people who stood by me and supported my children and me through our emotional struggles. Denice Kennedy moved into our home for six months, caring for all four children by helping them get ready for school, and driving or walking them to school each day. Walter and Wilma Stamps and their entire family embraced us and offered help by inviting us to dine with them on the first Easter that we experienced without Frank's presence.

Another dear friend recognized our need for a live-in housekeeper and interviewed a wonderful lady who managed household tasks, laundry, and cared for Brittany with exceptional dedication. Judy Donahue ran an outstanding daycare focused on high academic standards, providing Brittany with a nurturing environment three to four mornings a week. Anita Hoekstra, Francesca's first-grade teacher who had also experienced childhood loss of her father, provided invaluable support in helping Francesca navigate through her grief.

In addition, Mr. James Jones of Oceanside, CA, played a crucial role in supporting our son Alex. Mrs. Karen Mitchell and high school counselor Mrs. Ellisor were inspirations and invaluable aids to our oldest daughter Nina. I am deeply grateful to them and many others in our community who selflessly gave their time and resources to support our family through the overwhelming stages of grief. I will always cherish their kindness.

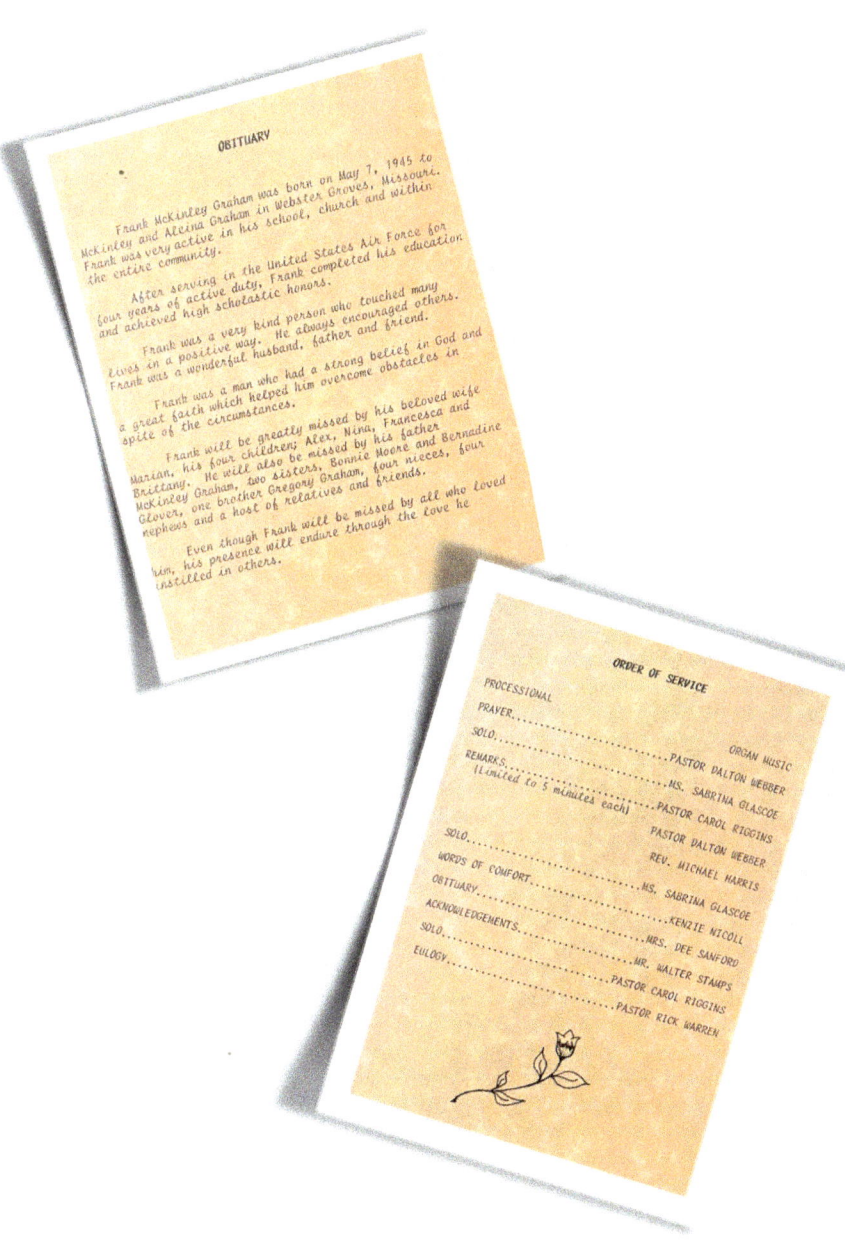

CHAPTER 19

THE SECOND PROMISE AT WIDOWHOOD

Frank's sister, Bernadine, called me to say that she and her husband, Tom, were on their way to help with the difficult task of clearing out Frank's closet. It contained a large collection of professional business suits, sport jackets, jogging gear, dress shoes, athletic shoes, dress shirts, a variety of ties, cufflinks, caps, and other accessories. This was emotionally challenging for me, as I often found comfort in hugging his clothes and remembering him by the scent of his favorite cologne or the memories associated with each outfit. However, with time passing, I knew it was time to close this chapter and move forward.

Bernadine and Tom's organized approach made the task much easier than I could have managed alone. Some of the men from our church were grateful to receive items from Frank's wardrobe. "Mr. Graham was always well-dressed and had excellent taste, just like he chose a beautiful wife!" remarked Mr. Leyva. We also donated a portion of the clothing and accessories to Goodwill and AmVets. When the closet was finally empty, tears flowed freely.

Suddenly, Nina burst into my room, her voice filled with fear and desperation. "Mom, what are we going to do now? Who will provide for us and take care of us now that Dad is gone? How will we pay for our house?" she cried out. I paused, recalling the promise I had made to her when she was just a baby in her bassinet.

In that moment, I remembered the words from John 5:8 when Jesus commanded, "Arise, take up your bed and walk!" It was time to fulfill my promise, not just to Nina but to all my children. With trembling hands and emotional exhaustion, I gathered my strength and stood tall, responding firmly, "I will take care of this family!

Our Family After Their Father Died

With God's help, I will provide for us, and I will raise all of you to be successful, in the name of Jesus!"

The promise I made filled me with determination, revving up my work ethic and pushing my mind into high gear. I took immediate action, moving forward without hesitation.

There was no turning back now. I embarked on a mission to fulfill that promise, to find a way to provide for my children.

Without God, I realized I was nothing—He runs everything, and I simply move within His plan. I trusted that He would guide me, as always. While returning to AT&T was an option, being a widow with four children meant I couldn't commit to business travel. This obstacle couldn't be overlooked. I needed a job or business that offered a high income, health insurance, as well flexibility to work from home to be available for school activities, PTA meetings, etc.

It took me a while to realize that the perfect opportunity was right in my home—literally, in a guest closet. One night, due to insomnia, I felt compelled to explore. Around 2:00 AM, I went downstairs and opened the living room closet. A large maroon leather portfolio fell out, containing a whiteboard and easel for professional presentations. On the shelves were binders filled with Frank Graham's handwritten instructions and business plans. Inspirational books by authors like Zig Ziglar, David Schwartz, Robert Schuller, Napoleon Hill, Tom Hopkins, and others lined the closet, alongside numerous audio cassette tapes from training seminars.

For the remainder of the night, I delved into the business plan, meticulously practicing the presentation on the whiteboard. Frank Graham, a shrewd and intelligent businessman, had endorsed this venture, lending it credibility in my eyes. I was driven by a deep-seated determination to succeed. Thank God for this opportunity—a brand new career blessing!

Over the next few weeks, our cassette player seemed to be running non-stop. Every time the car started, my children and I absorbed knowledge and motivation from various speakers on those tapes. Our car quickly transformed into a mobile university!

One Sunday, near the end of the service, Pastor Mark Griffo felt compelled by the Lord to call all business owners and aspiring entrepreneurs to the altar for prayer. I wondered if this was a confirmation from God. About six business owners responded. Standing beside me was a man who owned a construction business specializing in building classroom modules for school districts. I stood alone, seeking a blessing for my fledgling Direct Sales business. Pastor Griffo prayed fervently, asking God to bless my business so abundantly that UPS trucks would deliver products across the country, bringing prosperity.

Before long, that prayer was answered, and I am deeply grateful. God brought talented individuals into my life, people of integrity whose support was indispensable in achieving success. Together, we built a thriving organization, fostering mutually beneficial relationships and lasting friendships based on respect and trust.

Back in the day, when Frank Graham first recognized the potential of this business model, he became genuinely excited, especially after reading the Corporate Compendium in full. My initial response was, "Frank, it may sound appealing, but I didn't work hard to earn my B.S. degree and MBA to sell soap for anyone!" Thankfully, Frank saw past my initial resistance and persisted. He understood that regardless of how good a job one has at AT&T, it's crucial to seek opportunities that offer residual income—where you continue to earn even when you're not actively working.

He explained how McDonald's franchises operated, where franchisees earned from every hamburger sold, whether they were physically present or not. He illustrated through diagrams how building a Direct Selling Network, as outlined in the business model, could lead to a substantial six-figure income based on residuals earned even while we slept. Frank emphasized, "This is how you build a business that pays beyond your own time and effort. Unlike working for AT&T or any major corporation, where your income stops when you stop working or retire, a successful business can provide lasting financial security."

Our business team was fortunate to have Frank and Barbara Morales as mentors. Frank Morales was a high-level executive in the Data Processing Industry, while Barbara was listed in the Los Angeles Times as the 59th highest-paid female executive in California, serving as Vice President of a bank. Watching the Morales family, including their daughter Denice, achieve such success that they could retire from their jobs was not only impressive but also inspiring for all of us.

Photo with Mentors Frank and Barbara Morales

Building a successful business hinges on building a successful team. Among our key players were Dave and Brenda—Dave, a VP of an international company, and Brenda, a Communications major who worked for a local radio station. We also had Bob and Donna, highly successful entrepreneurs in the software industry, Vickie, a successful VP at one of the nation's largest banks, Greg and Christie, top executives in the paper industry, and the amazing leadership of The Martin and Associates Team.

Our team also included airplane pilots, physicians, engineers, teachers, and a diverse range of professionals from various backgrounds. The Lord blessed our team to become one of the most successful organizations in the region, all stemming from the seed of information left by Frank Graham in a closet. Truly, blessings can come from unexpected places!

Thankfully, the results over the years have far exceeded anything I could have imagined. One day, my daughter Francesca said, "Mom, I'm proud of you because you set goals and you reach them." These words alone set the tone for the example I set for my children and future generations. It's been said that "Your children will do what you do, not what you say." If I had remained depressed and helpless, it would have had a detrimental effect on their potential.

Becoming a successful business owner afforded me the opportunity to contribute tithes and offerings to the Lord, far exceeding my entire salary at AT&T. It's impossible to out-give God! By God's grace, the income from building the Direct Sales business allowed me to purchase a beautiful home in a great community to raise the children. It also provided for tuition at private Christian schools for Francesca and Brittany, and covered expenses for our children's participation in gymnastics, private figure skating lessons, cheerleading, volleyball, basketball, track & field, piano, and flute lessons. Not to mention the costs of regular beauty salon appointments.

Every year, the High Achievers Club offered all-expense-paid luxury vacations along with sizable bonuses to top achievers nationwide. Thanks to God and my team of business associates, I was blessed to attend these trips, and several achievers on our team also won these vacation awards.

Because I was a widow, it was always an honor for my sister Beverly to travel with me to the fabulous Achiever's Club destinations. One year, my dear friend Audra Popp joined me on the trip to Maui, Hawaii. Audra and her wonderful husband Larry had always been supportive of Frank and me. They continued to stand by our family long after he passed away, offering help wherever they could. They were especially supportive of my son Alex, whose best friends were their sons. This family was truly one of the kindest I have ever been blessed to know. Today, the Popp family members are also walking around in heaven with Frank Graham.

Losing such dear friends was a great loss for us on earth, and it took a great deal of time to recover psychologically from this emotional blow. But with God, all things are possible.

Reviews Are Gold to Authors:
Would you consider leaving a review on Amazon?

CHAPTER 20

FAITH AND HOPE

For the past 27 years I have been married to Stephen Ulrich, a very kind and caring man who is devoted to the Lord Jesus Christ. He is such a loyal husband who is extremely supportive of everything I do. Our entire family loves and accepts him. Our grandchildren affectionately call him GPS - Grand Pa Steve!

In this day and age, it is practically unheard of to witness the blessing of two marriages where the bride and groom share their first kiss at the altar! This miracle was witnessed before God when our daughters Francesca and her husband Kenneth married in 2007, and again in 2011 when Brittany and her husband Dak were united in Holy Matrimony. My first-born, Nina, and her husband Herman recently celebrated 33 years of marriage. All three families place the Lord Jesus Christ at the center of their marriages, and their children are raised with the virtues of honoring the Lord by putting Him first in their lives.

I am deeply grateful that by God's grace, my children have a strong foundation. Despite the challenges of raising them after their father's death, they have become children to be very proud of by any standard.

From an educational standpoint, it was a tremendous blessing to see them walk across the stage to receive BS in Business Administration degrees, graduating Magna Cum Laude. Their father, Frank Graham, would have been filled with admiration for what his children accomplished if he could have been present at each event.

High Tea with My 3 Wonderful Daughters

Looking toward the sky, I can truly say to Frank Graham that I have kept the promise I made to him posthumously: "Frank, your life will not be in vain. I promise to continue raising our children to be the best they can be." Thank you, Frank, for your outstanding fatherhood and the legacy you left behind. Thank you for taking us to church and helping our entire family grow closer to the Lord. Thank you for encouraging me to read the Bible and have daily devotions. Thank you for being the exemplary role model you were while on this earth.

Thank you for the everlasting love you showed to me and the children. Thank you for the respect and constant edification you displayed toward me. Thank you for being the glue that held our family together during tough times, when I wanted to walk away from it all. Thank you for your patience, understanding, and encouragement.

I remember, Frank, when people used to ask you how many children you had, you would jokingly tell them, "I have four children and Marian!" I always chuckled because I knew exactly what you meant. It took great patience on your part to handle this complex woman whom you married, nearly seven years younger and less wise than your advanced wisdom. Thank you for teaching me how to handle life, finances, and business. Thank you forever for being the leader I could willingly respect and follow.

It has taken many years of prayer and therapy for our son, Alex. When his father died, he felt like a part of him died with him. "Dad was all that I had left and now he is gone," cried Alex. Gifted and talented beyond measure, I encouraged Alex to move forward and live up to the God-given potential he possessed.

When his father was alive, they were active together in Alex's cub scout troop and baseball league. Alex dreamed of becoming an aeronautical engineer. Additionally, the director of the Orange County choir recognized Alex's outstanding singing voice and encouraged him to try out for the All-American Boys Choir. By the time Alex turned 16, his voice was so full and rich that he sounded like an opera star!

I recall saying to him, "Alex, it's hard to believe you're 16 already. You're almost grown up!"

"I don't want to grow up!" said Alex.

Hearing the pain in his voice was heartbreaking. He didn't want to grow up because he hoped it was all a nightmare or just a dream that his father was truly gone and not coming back.

He missed all the wonderful times he had with Frank and couldn't accept that those times with his father had come to an end. Sadly, Alex never had closure because he was visiting friends after school on the day his father died and never got a chance to say goodbye. To this day, Alex has not come to grips with the loss of Frank.

There is a God in heaven who recognizes Alex's struggles here on earth. God will never give up on Alex Graham, and neither will I. Frank Graham instilled so much within the genius DNA of Alex Graham, and with God's grace and mercy, someday it will all come to fruition. In all of this, my faith and hope in God is unwavering.

LIFE TODAY

Four Generations of Our Family Living The American Dream

CONCLUSION

Thank you for reading this book. It is my hope and prayer that you have gleaned something from my story that has inspired you to reach the dreams and goals you desire in your own life.

I want to leave you with four pillars of success that were weaved throughout my story for you to use to launch your life of resilience.

Nina and Marian

1. Awareness (without awareness you cannot grow)
    - Realize that God loves you and desires to walk with you through your life circumstances.
    - Your situation does not define you
    - Where you are today, does not have to be where you are tomorrow
    - Someone else's opinion of you does not have to be your reality

2. Education (formal or informal, as it relates to your goals)
   - Your education is a foundation of your destiny
   - Learn all you can to get where you want to go
   - Find good mentors and listen to them

3. Action (education without follow-through is meaningless)
   - One small step is the first step
   - Take the necessary steps each day
   - Action turns your education into reality

4. Independence (is much better than dependence)
   1. Become a "fisherwoman" (see chapter 11)*
   2. Stand on your own two feet
   3. Trust in God to guide you along the path

May you be blessed with much success on your journey!

You can connect with me at:
https://linktr.ee/WingsofResilienceforLife

EPILOGUE

Since the writing of this book, our dear Son Alex Graham, tragically lost his life, and he is now in Heaven with Frank Graham, his earthly father, and the Lord Jesus Christ. Our family feels the loss of their earthly presence to be extremely difficult.

Napoleon Hill once said, "Behind every adversity is a seed for greater benefit." While Alex's tragic death was heartbreaking, he left behind an amazing son and daughter, William and Akasha. We feel so blessed that they are in our lives.

BIBLE VERSES I STOOD ON

In the next few pages I am going to share with you some of the Bible verses that have encouraged me through all the various trials that I went through. I hope and pray that the words of each verse from the Bible will be helpful to you as well.

Being confident of this, that He who began a good work in you will carry it on to completion until the day of Christ Jesus.

-Philippians 1:6

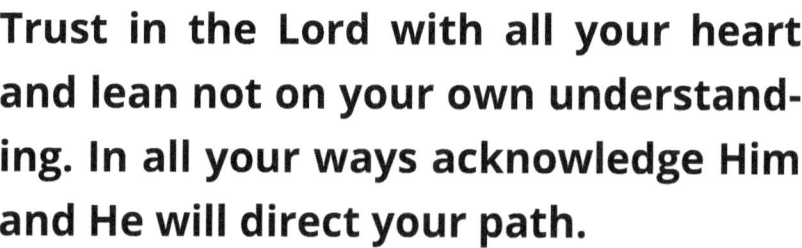

Trust in the Lord with all your heart and lean not on your own understanding. In all your ways acknowledge Him and He will direct your path.

-Proverbs 3:5-6

Be strong and of good courage, fear not, nor be afraid of them: for the Lord thy God, He will never leave you nor forsake you.

-Deuteronomy 31:6

And we know that all things work together for good to them that love God, to them who are the called according to His purpose.

-Romans 8:28

If we confess our sins, He is faithful and just and will forgive our sins and cleanse us from all unrighteousness.

-1 John 1:9

Now Faith is the substance of things hoped for, and the evidence of things not seen.

-Hebrews 11:1

Jabez cried out to the God of Israel. Oh, that you would bless me indeed and enlarge my territory! Let your hand be with me, and keep me from harm so that I will be free from pain, And God granted his request.

-1Chronicles 4:10

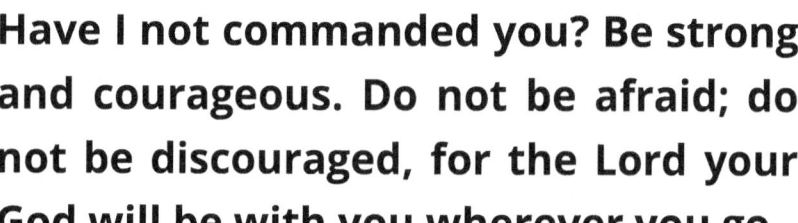

Have I not commanded you? Be strong and courageous. Do not be afraid; do not be discouraged, for the Lord your God will be with you wherever you go.

-Joshua 1:9

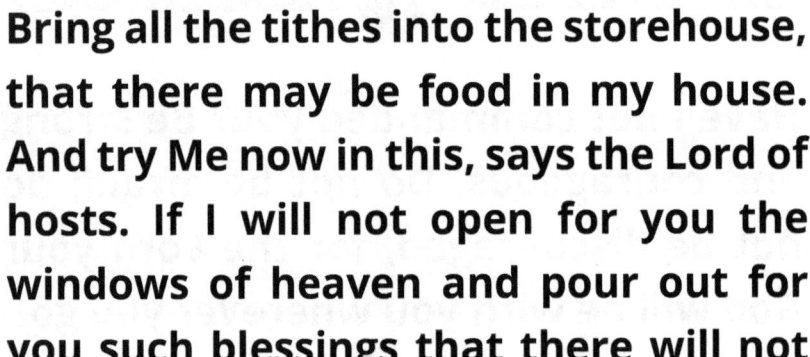

Bring all the tithes into the storehouse, that there may be food in my house. And try Me now in this, says the Lord of hosts. If I will not open for you the windows of heaven and pour out for you such blessings that there will not be room enough to receive it.

-Malachi 3:10

Therefore I tell you, whatever you ask for in prayer, believe that you have received it and it wills be yours.

-Mark 11:24

> **For I know the plans I have for you, declares the Lord. Plans to prosper you and not to harm you. Plans to give you hope and a future.**
>
> -Jeremiah 29:11

For He will command His Angels concerning you to guard you in all ways

— Psalm 91:11

DOWNLOAD YOUR FREE GIFT!

Read this guide I put together for you, to help you discover the top 5 ways to become more resilient, so you can build the life of your dreams.

Download it at: https://linktr.ee/WingsofResilienceforLife

ABOUT THE AUTHOR

Marian is a Christ-follower, business professional, speaker, wife, mother and grandmother.

Marian believes in moving towards progress and results without focusing on limitations, as well as how important it is to take immediate action once your goal has been set.

For over 30 years she has helped and inspired hundreds of people to set goals and achieve their expected outcomes.

She earned a Bachelor of Science degree from Washington University in St. Louis, and an MBA degree from Webster University.

Marian enjoys spending quality time with family and friends, traveling, hiking, horseback riding, singing, health and fitness, water aerobics, attending sporting events and Symphony Orchestra concerts.

To connect with Marian or book her for a speaking engagement, visit: https://linktr.ee/WingsofResilienceforLife

www.ingramcontent.com/pod-product-compliance
Lightning Source LLC
Chambersburg PA
CBHW050905160426
43194CB00011B/2298